My 44 Wives

A true story of multiple personality

by George A. Lareau

SUFI GEORGE BOOKS
TUCSON

ISBN 978-1-885570-17-8

Sufi George Books: http://sgbooks.sufigeorge.net

Dedication

This book is dedicated to the men who love the women who are afflicted with Multiple Personality Disorder; to those who suffer from MPD; to all abuse survivors; and to Rebecca, one of the great loves of my life.

On Christmas day, I met a girl. She has given me joy and anguish. I welcome the joy.

She is a Catholic-confused girl whose life has been intolerable for her. She has difficulty letting go of misery because it is such a familiar companion to her. She offers me moments that make my life seem completely fulfilled. And she yanks such moments away from me, making me wish I had never met her.

I have allowed myself, so far, to be battered back and forth in this way. I have told myself that the joyful moments are merely expensive, but I am becoming unwilling to spend myself so carelessly.

She offers me a contest rather than a relationship. We play on her terms alone, and she retains the right to suddenly shift the terms. My part in the contest is to read her mind so well that I can cope with these shifts, or else suffer the consequences.

She sees this as an agreeable arrangement, one which

will continue for the rest of our lives. I find it disagreeable, and I want to display behaviors that she finds disagreeable so that she will stop. I know this is no suitable answer.

She is suffering the consequences of abuse, yet she abuses me, and I don't know if she realizes that she is perpetuating abuse. And I don't know what will happen if I stop allowing her to abuse me.

I had thought that it would be enjoyable to help her, but so far she has no idea whatever of what help I can offer. So far, she has interpreted me only in the same terms that she uses to interpret herself. And as a result, she can't conceive of letting go of what she has, because she can't see anything better.

She only feels threatened by the possibility. It is no fun trying to help her. And as she is, she is abusive to me. I have less appetite for abuse than I once had—I thought I had finally escaped from abuse. Now I have to wonder if I am willing to tolerate more of it, or face the risky and unpleasant chore of helping her to change, with little likelihood of good results.

Perhaps she is so accustomed to abuse, and to reacting with abuse, that she is prone to interpret my most innocent behaviors as abusive, and she retaliates with abuse.

I have told her that she must learn to forgive, but she cannot see this as a growth area that is possible for her, and is completely disinclined to approach it. Yet, until she tackles this successfully, she will see abuse surrounding her, and she will continue to be abusive herself.

She sees herself as a saint who somehow succeeded spiritually without learning about forgiveness, and has no interest in making up the deficiency. She clutches to her sainthood with a desperation, and its mantle does not rest comfortably on her shoulders.

She has steered me remarkably away from my purposes, and I have cooperated, on the presumption that I can afford, even benefit from, a temporary diversion.

Yet, it is beginning to appear that my sense of mission with regard to teaching and writing cannot be compatible with this relationship. I was willing to surrender these objectives for the reward of this relationship, which would have been price enough. But there are so many additional prices that the bargain becomes a questionable one. I am reconsidering, I am thinking that abuse is price enough, and that my purposes need not also be handed over. And yet the price remains too high.

Have I erred in creating this relationship? Have I, in providing myself with a magnificent test of my personal powers, hopelessly overwhelmed myself? At this moment, I have no eagerness about it. My fear of failure has mushroomed from the exile to which I had abandoned it. I have lost contact with my strength, or, perhaps, cannot access the vast amount of strength which this relationship requires. A week's supply is exhausted in a single day. It is a real mystery to me that it can go so fast.

This contest of a relationship has been my only occupation. I have given all of my energy to it, and it has not been enough. It is dark. This is a moment of total rejection. Were I writing during a moment when I had her total trust, my words would measure a mile high.

Yet what is the value of a trust so fragile that it can

unexpectedly vanish absolutely? It does not seem only to have been misplaced or redirected, but to have been annihilated altogether. It pulls my heart out by the arteries.

She does not yet see me as a human, but only as a symbol, a sort of social savior. She has my role completely described in her mind, and has not consulted me about it. She is not yet aware that I can have feelings of my own, but attends only to her own feelings, and looks for their reflection from me, and asks that I attend to her feelings only, in disregard of my own.

She is, of course, the center of her universe, but cannot see that I have a universe of my own. She sees only that I am a part of hers. I feel she wants to swallow me completely, and make of me only what she imagines for me.

I am her testimony that she lives in the real world, and she has no interest in learning of my world. She has attempted to make a gift of herself to me, but cannot figure out how to do it, for she takes it all back at the slightest hint of provocation. I am unable to take the gift seriously.

It is rather like a loan that is payable in full on demand, over and over. I have become defensive about accepting it now. I can relate on those terms only if I have no feeling of investment in her on my part. But I don't want to withdraw my investment. I don't want to just surrender. I want to win.

I want her to stop canceling the relationship at a moment's notice. I want her to stop canceling the relationship period. Somehow, that requires more than the issue of trust. It requires an understanding of forgiveness, so that her past will stop coloring her present with abuse, so that things in the present will not be misinterpreted according to things in the past.

And it requires my constant and reliable forgiveness of her abuse. I don't know how I will be able to command that much energy. Solving that is my next task.

She will need a similar quantity of energy herself, and I will need to know where mine comes from, if I am to help her. I know that I know, but it seems I have temporarily forgotten. I feel like Samson, aware of my strength, but shorn.

I became angry with her for the first time last night. I had not thought that possible for me. But my energy was low. I cannot see the virtue of increasing my energy only to have it wantonly dissipated by her complete withdrawals from me. It is a signal for action, a warning alarm, that I should become angry with her. It is a death knell that I must view with fright. It is an indicator that I have been pulled down into an inferior level of consciousness, one which I had considered outgrown and abandoned.

It is real trouble for me, and is certainly trouble for the relationship. I feel that she, as my worthy opponent, is winning the first round, and that I had better stop belittling the magnitude of the challenge that she represents for me, and fortify myself for the most severe test I have ever faced.

I am wondering if there is anything else in my life that I should attend to first, by way of settling my affairs, in case I do not survive this contest. But God pity her if she should win, for we shall both have lost.

You are unfaithful to me. When you reject me, I feel as rejected as I would if you had slept with another man right alongside of me. The rejection is equivalent.

I'm a survivor, and when I lose you through those rejections, I begin looking for another friend. My trust in you is destroyed, and I want to find someone I can trust, someone who will accept me as her important person. Your rejections make me feel very unimportant to you, and very alone.

Maybe you can turn trust and rejection on and off as if they were switches, but I suffer when you do that, and I am not at all anxious to reestablish my trust in you and set myself up to be totally rejected again without any warning.

Yet, I don't want to lose you. My temptation is to find a tolerable middle ground, like saying to you, let's just be roommates.

When you reject me, I change my mind about marrying you. I'm willing to be your welfare plan in exchange for our companionship, but I don't want to lock myself into a relationship that involves continuing episodes of total rejection. I refuse to adjust to that. You must adjust to me, and be faithful to me.

Last night, I took her to see John Hartford who was performing at Harvard. John seemed tired, but he was great.

She was real bitchy, obviously so. John stared at her as he performed. My observation is that we began our relationship with a welcome and complete intimacy, but that it was possible only because I permitted her to control the relationship for the first week. Then, she had a flashback episode, and I began taking control. As she sensed that she was no longer in control, she retreated, and instead of relating directly to me, she created a role of wife and related to that. That was a step away from intimacy.

Currently, she has taken an additional step away by investing much less of herself in the role and simply retreating into herself. She knows that she is facing a frightening decision, and I am doing what I can to help her make the decision as early as possible, because it is very unpleasant to deal with the process.

I feel inhibited writing about it because I don't feel willing to share just anything and everything that I write. Intimacy has been set aside. I've told her everything that I've written here, but I still feel inhibited about writing it.

Yesterday, she felt a strong impulse to run away. She feels it is to her credit that she came home. Her activities—nothing abnormal in terms of load—had so exhausted her that she had nothing left for me. I told her this morning that this showed our relationship was at the bottom of her list of priorities.

I've told her that our relationship comes at a price, the price of letting go of her old self and becoming a part of us. She understands all of this, but experiences a great fear of letting go of her old self. I understand it

11

all, but that doesn't make it any easier for her.

She has been feeling used whenever I have been assertive. She has stopped giving herself, and feels taken. But she has taken herself, away from me. Her accusations are sullen. She does not seem to want relief from her negative feelings, and somehow seems to prefer to wallow in them.

It is not an easy thing for me to figure out how to help her. My approach currently is to increase the pressure on making a decision, but that is at the risk that she is unable to make a healthy decision.

I suppose I must find a way of making the decision for her, and making it acceptable to her, but how that can be done remains a mystery.

She is barely able to take the pressure of working three afternoons a week at her volunteer job. And she is thinking that she should work full-time for a year before beginning RN training—after completing the nursing assistant training. In her present state, she will not be able to handle the pressure of that training, and certainly not that of a full-time job.

Perversely, she is clutching to her present state, dead set on failure and defeat. Brains are not her problem. She is intellectually very capable. I see her problem as fear. Fear is conquered by knowledge. But she fears even knowledge, and that is a catch-22 situation.

If I could somehow manage to communicate to her the knowledge that emotions arc voluntary, it would be a great stride for her. If she could know that memories can be selected and controlled, that one is not at their mercy, it would help her a great deal. But she fears new knowledge, and clings to what she already knows as if it were her very life.

She was fairly strong when we met, and has been regressing more or less steadily. I have given her the freedom to do so, which she did not have before. That's the problem with freedom—it can be used or abused. And while she has made a few stabs at using it, she has done a much better job of abusing it.

Rather than capitalize on the opportunities for growth which freedom has provided to her, she has chosen to give new life to her old problems. She seems unaware that she has the ability to make such a choice, and permits her memories and emotions to control her.

I have consistently emphasized the use of her mind as a controlling mechanism, but she is easily overpowered, hence irrational. Unfortunately, she seems not to have a concept of what her life would be like if she should develop the use of her mind, and I find it difficult to make it seem appealing to her.

She gives advice to her friends as if she were some enlightened sage. She cannot handle our relationship, her job, her other relationships, or much of anything that goes into making up her days. She can't even handle the temperature or the noise of the radiator. Yet, she thinks she is able to give good advice. She is apparently afraid even of taking a good look at herself. A little less ego, a little more humility.

She has a curious habit of maximizing things. Her descriptions of things are usually exaggerated, and her vision of future plans are greatly blown-up. She seems to be trying to make things more real by making them overwhelming. She doesn't have an accurate understanding that ordinary reality is just that—quite ordinary.

The challenge continues. In the meantime, we live in an air of neutral suspense, wondering, both of us, about our progress and our outcome. We have stopped daring to be spontaneous and open about positive things, and have been emphasizing and dealing with negative things. Perhaps this is necessary work, but it is drudgery when it is not relieved by the happy intimacy which we have tasted.

I counsel her to let go of things because they are so important to her that they overwhelm her. She needs to let go of perfectionism, of her compulsion with time which makes her feel everything must be attended to right now, of her ideas of proper behavior which are unnatural to her, of her past hurts, of her rights, of her criticisms of trivia, of her fear of failure, trust, intimacy.

I encourage her to develop her potentials, to learn to assess herself and her behavior from a rational, rather than an emotional, viewpoint. I encourage her to attend to her positive emotions, rather than focus exclusively on the negative ones. She screams and bitches. I persist. It is an interesting challenge. I now understand the nature of the challenge well enough. Specific techniques are still coming in a little fuzzy, however.

It was Christmas day, a good day for meeting

Rebecca, for she was a gift of unimaginable fascination. I fell in love with her in an instant, just as she did with me. It took me all of the next week to adjust to it, to face up to it, really, and to do something about it. I called her up and invited her over. She brought me flowers.

She walked into my apartment and saw that it was very tiny, that there was one room with my sofa and desk, half of another room with a small table and refrigerator, and a door leading to the bathroom. Her first words were, "Where's your bed?" I liked that. It might have been innocent, but all the same it was what was on her mind.

"Oh, the couch is a hideabed," I explained to her.

Rebecca took charge. "Do you have any tea or wine?" she asked, not waiting for me to offer. I poured two glasses of red wine. I had two inexpensive but lovely wine glasses which I had been saving for such a time as this, and we drank red wine together, Rebecca sitting on the couch, me sitting next to her on the rickety armchair that I had dragged up from the storage room in the basement.

We talked about how we had met, how I had thrown a Christmas eve party for a number of the tenants in the building who had nowhere to go for Christmas, mostly alcoholics and crazies living out their lives in this rooming house whose new owner had not yet evicted them.

The party had moved to two other rooms in the course of the evening, and had resumed, without my knowledge, on Christmas day, in a room just down the hall. At a certain point, I got invited to join them, but there was this feeling that I wouldn't have been invited at all if it hadn't been for the fact that I had started the whole party thing that weekend, and had put a lot of money, for me, into food and drinks.

So it was my party that was responsible for getting me into that room where Rebecca was visiting with a friend who lived in the building. I walked into that room and saw Rebecca stretched out on the bed. She saw me walk into the room. It was the kind of magic that made us both retreat instantly, as if we had touched a warm burner which, while it felt good to the cold hand, was one of those acts that one was simply conditioned against doing.

But after a while, after watching each other out of the corners of our eyes, listening to each other speak to others, we looked fully at each other and smiled a frank, full, open smile that told us both that the conditioning was willingly being set aside. We were in love.

I put the flowers in some water. As soon as our small talk was over, small only in relation to what was to come next out of Rebecca's mouth, I sat speechless as I listened to an account of how much horror can be packed into a 27-year-old woman's life. She wanted me to know all of this up front; she wasn't pulling any punches, she knew that she and I were a miracle happening, and she felt it had to begin on a footing of complete, frank honesty.

She paused for just a few seconds, looked down into her glass of wine, and began speaking. Softly, in a breathy monotone. Detached, as if she were telling a story that bored her, yet it was clear enough that she simply couldn't afford, emotionally, to touch the feelings that the story contained.

I didn't know how to react. I sat and just listened. There was no doubt in my mind that she was telling the truth. Her first words were, "When I was four-and-a-half, my father raped me."

I glanced up at the bathroom doorway where I expected to see Rebecca at any moment since she was in the bathroom, and there was a flash of reflection off the corner of my glasses, a flash of amorphous substance, and I saw Rebecca's arm and part of her body as I would have seen her as she emerged from the bathroom, but instantly I knew that I was not making the correct perception and just as suddenly there was no Rebecca there.

This made me realize that I did see, if only for an instant, not what was there but what I expected to see. My expectation made a detailed interpretation of the mass of light that reflected from the edge of my glasses. And the interpretation remained visible to me for about the length of time it took for the reflection to whiz by my vision.

I saw what I expected to see. I was not immediately aware that I had been seeing what I expected to see; this had to occur to me, which makes me wonder about how much is going on that has not occurred to me.

Tonight, Francoise is coming over to join us for an Easter dinner. Francoise had breakfast with us this morning. We had difficulty finding a restaurant that was open and we ended up eating at Seven Stars and again at Dunkin Donuts.

I keep having fantasies about living as a family with Rebecca and Francoise. I tell myself not to encourage such a fantasy, but that does little good because it is such an attractive fantasy that I am helpless to resist thinking about it. Est-ce que c'est possible pour une homme aimer deux femmes at la meme temps avec tout son coeur? Je pense que oui.

Rebecca has gone to bed right after supper tonight. She was barely able to stay awake on the bus home. So I have toked up and am at my desk, jotting on my new computer setup. Francoise called earlier to ask about coming over this evening, but Rebecca was too tired to consider it. I wondered if it would be possible for Francoise and me to have coffee together.

And I've been fantasizing about seducing women left and right, women in the building, on the T, in other offices I can see into, any other women. I am at such a high sexual pitch that my appetite surrounds me like an aura. Being awake is being sexually charged from body memory of Rebecca. I would not be willing to admit any of these ideas to my mind except that I am toked. I love my sweet Rebecca.

A weekend passed, the first gorgeous weather weekend of the season. I bought a stereo tuner and speakers in celebration. We walked along the Charles, arm in arm. Rebecca's mother took us to Little Osaka for dinner to celebrate Rebecca's birthday. I got to meet Maggie, her cute, remote and forlorn sister.

I've been offered a $100 a week raise for the next fiscal year. That's substantial, and is enough for now. I'm thinking that it buys me a year of time during which I can prepare to live off my writing. It would be great to have a regular column a year from now, and to have a book coming out.

I have bits and pieces of time available for writing, and I guess I will have to put them to use rather than wait for clear extended periods. It is nice to sit here at the foot of the bed, typing on my little keyboard, listening to classical music on my headset while Rebecca sleeps. We have made very sweet love, and she is off to sleep and will get up in the wee hours to study.

I first became aware that I am losing my mind two days ago, when I was in search of something, had looked directly at the scene that contained it without seeing it, recalled the scene and saw that I had allotted empty space to the sought item without a second thought, and that it had been there all along.

Now, I suppose this is a common enough occurrence, but I was without my mind during this incident specifically because I did not care about the blocking out that I had done. There is much these days that I do not care about, and these days I am happy. I am absolutely serene when I am high, lazily stretched in bed with Rebecca, listening to good music on the stereo, and making love with my lovely companion's body. It is a life devoutly to be wished. It is what all of the hours are supporting, what they are pointed toward.

It's the good loving that keeps me mystified, and when it gets set aside for a few days or more, then I wake up and see that I am living in an arrangement I don't like because it costs me my freedom.

Knowing this, I yet prefer to be mystified; its only hazard is waking up from it, and it is such a delightful garden in which to be lost.

But, awakened, I seriously ask myself if this is such a practical or beneficial way to live. The question is: Will I be more satisfied when I look back upon my life if I see that I passed much of it lost in love; or that I stayed practical. And it's a toss-up.

The plain fact is, when I am not so mystified, I am depressed. I am depressed, whether or not it shows on the surface of my life. It is an ever-present undercurrent ready to push its way to the surface.

We call it spring because it looks like spring and it smells like spring. What may escape us is the utter audibility of spring in the city, that symphony of sounds seemingly awakened by the opening of windows. And it is not the mere opening of windows, not the mere entry of those back-orchestra rhythms: the monotony of the air conditioners, heaving slowly; the slower rhythm of traffic flowing and alternately slowing for the light; the punctuation of the trolley passing, the occasional siren sounding, the shouting pedestrian, the clang of the dumpster, the gulls; it is not only that opening the windows permits this orchestration to enter, but that the opening of many windows lends to the crescendo the melodies of many radios and televisions, conversations, an occasional vacuum cleaner, the clink of dishes being washed, all manner of sounds which had been hidden within the walls of wintry brick, now loosed in the symphony of spring.

I gave Rebecca an engagement diamond, and she gave me an engagement gold chain which I've worn since. We've signed a lease for a much larger apartment, a one-bedroom up the street at 1292 Commonwealth, for September 1st.

I've been in the early stages of developing a word processing business. Rebecca finished nursing assistant training with flying colors and has interviewed two places. Mitch has become my supervisor because no one else knew what to do with me. There was a first floor fire in the building one night. I have gained weight and am trying to figure out how to avoid that. I haven't written much of anything for a long time. I have been in heaven, high in the arms of my darling with good music in the background. I love Boston. I really will be a good metaphysical teacher someday.

Her psychiatrist was intrigued. And no wonder, for how often is a scientist such as she confronted with a blazing bit of superstitious nonsense, a bit so incontestably real and present that it is indisputably there?

She was telling her psychiatrist of the interesting coincidence. She was moving into a new apartment, and it was the same apartment where her parents lived when she was born.

Had she known the address beforehand? No, not really. It was six months since she had shown her birth certificate to me, which showed that address. Nor had we paid it any attention then. Later, her mother mentioned that she had lived not far from here, but somehow it hadn't been an item of curiosity, and no, the building had not been identified.

Had she chosen that address when she was apartment hunting? Did she select the building, perhaps unconsciously? No. In fact, I had chosen the rental agency and had specified a preference only for a Commonwealth Avenue address. The agency handles some 5,000 apartments which include much of Comm Ave. And while it was the first of the three apartments we were shown, it was the only one that qualified according to the personal checklist of features we had earlier agreed upon. Large, for a one-bedroom, first floor. On Comm Ave. Cheap, and this was only $400 a month, heated. Stove with an oven. Sink with a drain board. Both were lacking in our present apartment.

When did she confirm the address as that of her birthplace? Before signing the lease? No. It hadn't even occurred to her to check. I asked her, a few nights after signing the lease, to get her birth certificate to see if our new address was anywhere close to her birthplace. It was; it was her birthplace.

The psychiatrist would have relaxed if this were happening inside the patient's head, for such a blazing symbol would not be at all difficult to interpret. The desire, the need, for rebirth. But it was happening in the wrong place. It was happening out there in reality. And she was intrigued by that.

I am a brand new character in a story, this story, and I don't know much about myself yet. I know that I raped my four-and-a-half year old daughter in a brutal, vicious manner, but I don't know why I did it or why I did it that way. And no, I now decide, I am not remorseful, only curious about myself.

I loved my little daughter, and delighted in playing with her. Yes, I tried to hide away those thoughts of incest, but they had, and have, strength. I am not, then, altogether surprised that I should actually have done it. I wonder, rather, why I did it in that awful way?

I can imagine that I might have concocted a scheme in which I was so horrible with my daughter, so much in contrast with my normal self, that I would escape detection simply because no one would believe her story. And I could console my daughter for having had a "bad dream." And, finding that no one would believe her, she would stop making the effort of telling someone, and I would be home free.

Perhaps, I thought then, if I brandish a kitchen knife and make horrible threats, and perhaps even touch her sensitive parts with the knife to reinforce her terror, then I will be especially unbelievable, for no one who knows me would ever dream of suspecting that I was capable of such behavior.

Then again, perhaps I secretly studied hypnotism back then, for this is thirty years ago that I am describing, and hypnotism was not yet a respectable subject, and perhaps I learned that there are three ways to hypnotize a person: deep relaxation, authority, and shock. And suppose I had figured out that I could hypnotize my little daughter so that she wouldn't remember that I had molested her, and that the safest technique was shock, and since this was a highly risky business, and I wanted every edge of safety, I used shock.

And what could be more shocking to a little girl than to see her Daddy menacing her with a knife and hurting her body with it? And it would have worked—she wouldn't remember a thing about it, and I would be safe. I suppose this is a possible explanation of why I did it the way I did it, but somehow I don't find it singularly satisfactory.

It may have been that I was an actual example of a real life Dr. Jekyll and Mr. Hyde, that I had a hidden personality that perpetrated this rape on my own daughter. Given the right opportunity, and what better than to have one's pregnant wife in hospital delivering and to be at home alone with the child, the Mr. Hyde emerges, raging with pent-up anger, genuinely shocking my daughter into speechlessness, so horrifying the behavior that she cannot absorb it, and she buries it deeply in her mind.

Can I prevent Mr. Hyde from seriously harming her? If I allow Mr. Hyde to do this deed for me, so that my hands remain clean, will my little daughter be safe? If not safe from any harm at all, at least safe from serious injuries such as broken bones or ruptured organs?

She cried so much that Mr. Hyde struck her head severely against the headboard to shut her up, and then like a coward he vanished, leaving me to pick up the pieces, leaving it up to me to get her to the emergency room, her little body limp in a coma.

I am at work after a sleepless night. Rebecca is going through a crazy period, on the heels of another. She is feeling swallowed up by me and is afraid of disappearing. She refused to make love with me last night. I am so weary of dealing with her episodes that I am prepared to call off the engagement and give her the freedom she wants to enjoy her newfound personhood.

She has been working for three weeks now and comes home each day too exhausted to deal with me, combined with an apparent resentment toward the commitments of our relationship.

Her feelings of being overwhelmed and of disappearing have come up repeatedly during our relationship, but the smooth and loving periods in between episodes seem to be shorter and less frequent, which makes the relationship very taxing for me. I love her, but am prepared to give her back to herself and let her go.

I realize that I am demanding in our relationship, but I don't want to content myself with a relationship that only hovers around total commitment to each other. We have that potential, it seems, except for her apparent fear of it. That fear has been recurrent, and strongly so, and I am fatigued from dealing with it.

I am going to ask for the rings back tonight, ask for reimbursement for her uniforms, and ask her to pay her third of the expenses. (Francoise lives with us and pays a third.) She can remain as a roommate until she decides to move out. I will try to lose myself in my writing for a time.

How does a man face the need to grow? How do I relinquish power in my relationship with Rebecca, develop respect for her personhood and freedom as an individual? How do I surrender the claim to all of Rebecca's free time that we are able to spend together, allow her to have outside friendships of her own? How can I stop possessing this woman?

This is my growth task.

My reaction in the previous journal entry did not face this unwillingness to surrender control over her. I saw it as all or nothing, and opted for nothing. I've been thinking that it would be easier to find someone new I could control rather than face my growth task. And the thought occurred to me that this would provide me with an endless series of relationships, helping my mates to grow until they outgrew that sort of relationship.

I have been quite depressed over this. Is depression a

reaction to refusing to grow? I do not welcome this growth, for it steals power away from me.

Granting power to others in my life has frequently led to abuse of me in various ways. At about age 21, I vowed not to be a feeling person, not to extend myself emotionally to others beyond my power to control the situation, in order to protect myself, for I had been badly hurt. Now, in order to grow, I must reconsider this decision and become an emotional risk-taker.

I have felt very abused by Rebecca, many times, but perhaps it has been because she resented my control, my power. And I have suffered from my perceived abuse. It may be that my earlier decision set me up to suffer from protecting my power instead of protecting my emotions, and that I have simply swapped one risk for another.

My quest for intimacy has probably been fed by the starvation effect of restricting my emotional expressions. My demands on Rebecca for a degree of intimacy that satisfies me have been suffocating to her. I cherish the idea of a relationship so intimate that the only fundamental reality is that relationship. But I have apparently exercised excessive domination in my attempt to insure that our relationship remain that intimate.

Dear Rebecca,

I have loved you to the best of my ability, which has been the greatest loving I have ever felt toward another person. It has not been adequate for you. I feel that my love has been tested too severely, and that while you have been seeking reassurance regarding my love for you on the one hand, you have also been systematically destroying it.

You presented me with an ultimatum. Either I had to change in accordance with your change into someone with personhood, or else the relationship simply could not continue. You presented this to me believing firmly that I was unwilling and unable to change.

You may tell yourself that you were giving me an opportunity to "shape up," but in fact you gave me very little choice, just enough to make it appear that it was I who was ending the relationship, not you. You designed it so that you would not have to bear any responsibility for ending the relationship. In a word, you were deliberately ending the relationship.

You are a man-hater. This is something we have discussed in the past, and you certainly have good reason to hate men. I was naive enough to think that it didn't apply to me, that I was somehow an exception to your feelings, that I was perhaps the only man you could find acceptable. But you have repeatedly attempted to abort our relationship, each time causing me severe grieving.

Perhaps my tolerance of these behaviors has in itself been a frustration for you, making you wonder how in the world you will ever get out of this relationship and manage to hurt me enough in the process to fulfill your inner mandate that men should be punished.

I have been very conscientious in helping you build your self-esteem and self-confidence. Perhaps I have done too good a job, because you are on what looks like an ego trip. Perhaps I was overly zealous in this, and helped you believe that you are more than you are. Ordinarily, this is beneficial, but in your case I think it is dangerous to your life plans.

You are behaving immaturely in your new found personhood, simply because it is a new thing to you. I'm sure you feel that you are standing on top of a mountain—you are self-sufficient now, certified, employed. But in real world terms, you have only climbed to the top of a foothill.

You have exited the ranks of the unemployable, which is a big step, but that has put you into a new arena, where you are employed at one of the lowest possible ranks, at a wage that is minimal to say the least. On your own, you won't be able to save up the money you need to go to nursing school. You will be stuck exactly where you are unless you realize that nursing school can only be accomplished with the help and support of a mate.

Thus, you are not free of mates; you still need one, if only for practical purposes. In view of your man-hating nature, I suspect that you will eventually find a satisfactory lesbian relationship.

The growth that you stipulate as a requirement for me, that of becoming less possessive toward you with greater respect for your status as an individual, is a goal which I acknowledge as good. That is, I agree that I would be a better person for having made that change within myself.

However, I have assessed the work involved in making the change, and it is not an easy task for me, desirable though it may be. I can suffer my way through the change with intense introspection and reorganization, but it will be a tortuous process for me, and I won't be fit to live with for the duration, And, that process appears to be one which would require weeks and weeks.

There is a slower but more palatable way of approaching the change, and that is to act as if I had made the change in myself, and allow it to gradually become internalized. This might work in terms of providing us with a temporarily more satisfactory relationship for the next few months, but unless we should happen to rediscover each other and fall in love with each other in a new way, it is only an expedient, and I would expect you to announce at some point that it wasn't working and that you were leaving. I am adopting that expectation, because I don't even really like this new you. And that makes me anxious to get on with my own life.

Because I still love the remnants of the old Rebecca, some of which are still visible in you, I am willing to give patching up the relationship a try, but I doubt that is what you really want, and I have no hopes for it doing anything more than making life a little less miserable for the two of us until you move out.

I know that a good sex life is very important to you, and we can use this "trial process" as a subterfuge for reintroducing sex into our lives, "kidding" ourselves along that we are trying to patch up our relationship, but inside we will know that this is simply an arrangement to satisfy sexual needs until you are in a position to move about and call our patching up experiment a failure.

I expect that you will find this suggestion very offensive because it is grossly materialistic. But should you manage to find it agreeable, then I want you to know that in this trial process, I will not be your servant or slave; you must stand on the two feet of your own personhood. Nor will I be your banker; it is important for you to discover the limits of your current status, to be more realistic about it.

At this point, I don't really care how you decide this issue. I am willing to go along with it if you are, and I can live without it just as easily. My sex drive is also strong, but my self-esteem is also very strong and I don't "need" to have sex with you ever again.

In your heart, I'm sure that there is a strong part of you that doesn't want to lose our relationship, but it is not a strong enough part of you to compete with your man-hatred. Your next growth area is learning the importance of cooperative relationships, because right now you feel omnipotent, and that is hazardous because you are not. You are only stronger than you were, which is very good, but you need to acknowledge its practical limits.

I reacted to one of your comments by noting that you wanted me to love you as if I were Jesus. I think there is truth in that, and I think that it is an impossible expectation on your part, deliberately so at some deep level. It is a way of making me appear too inferior to hold up my end of the relationship; it is a way of making it appear that it is a failure on my part that is responsible for the break-up of our relationship.

After nine months of living together, you know me rather well (as I know you rather well), and you know exactly where to hit me to get the effect you want. I hope you will face this squarely so that someday you can have and enjoy a happy relationship with someone, man or woman, me or someone else.

I am grateful to you for having enriched my life, although at a high cost to me emotionally. Having experienced a relationship like we once had, I would never feel a need to do it again. This means that, should we make a serious attempt to get our relationship back together, which I think is unlikely, it will be on terms which I will participate in describing.

31

For example, I do not want to be subjected to any more of your ultimatums. Either our relationship will unfold on the basis of a cooperative and mutual dependency, or it will not unfold at all.

Either you face up to your need, the need of most humans, to accept a degree of dependency on someone else, or you go it alone. If this seems to be a legitimate condition for a new relationship, then I will certainly be helpful and tolerant as you work on this growth area. Again, I do not have high hopes for success, but then again, you have always been full of surprises and I will give it a chance if you want to tackle it.

I feared her power to destroy me. My fear left me emasculated, castrated, impotent. But with a few puffs of weed, my head straightened out. I said, so she can destroy me—will fearing that make it any less terrible? I said, she's not destroying me right now, so why react to it right now? I said, my fear makes me weak, but I can be strong simply by facing down the fear and presenting my vulnerability to her with all of my love.

In the first few months of our relationship, I said to her, "Why do I have the feeling that I have been put in your life to make your last days more comfortable?"

I was so saddened by the nature of her life as it had

been up to the moment I met her that it seemed unnatural for her to be experiencing happiness with me. I loved making her happy and did many little things to make her happy. But it was such an ill-fitting experience in the context of her life that it made me wonder how our cosmic benefactor had justified it in his overall plans for her. It gave me so much joy to see her happy and I marveled at how very happy she was. At times, of course.

I had voiced that sentence to myself once before and this time it came out. It didn't shock her when I said it. She looked at me with an amused smile as we walked on some errand. And I shook the thought off.

When I came home today, there was a note from her on the table. She asked to be awakened at 7:00 because she didn't get to bed until noon. She had a doctor's appointment this morning that had been set by a form letter saying there had been some irregular result from her pap smear. We talked about it for the letter had worried her. I tried to reassure her on the one hand but felt duty-bound by honesty to point out that she is statistically a good candidate for cervical cancer because two of the correlates are multiple sex partners and sex early in life.

We dropped the subject and I forgot about it until yesterday when I remembered that her appointment was today. I must have reassured myself, if not Rebecca, for I had no fears for her. In her note is the cryptic line: "doctor's visit difficult." And I fear.

I fear for her for the fear she must be feeling. I fear losing her. I don't know what is implied by cervical cancer if that in fact is what was difficult; yet, I don't know what else to consider. Does it mean a hysterectomy? Does that end our plans for children? Will her life be in continued danger? Will we be alone in the world with only each other to cling to? Yes, I am fearing many things.

And I am especially wondering about my early thought that I am enhancing her last days. Why did I think that? Was it some kind of premonition? I'm trying to remember what I was feeling or what thoughts or events came just prior, but nothing comes.

Why did I say it aloud? I must have thought it seriously enough that I wanted to register it aloud, imprint the question, the idea, on the fabric of my life. Not because I liked the thought, only that I took it seriously as a thought.

It is a little later. She got up to go to the bathroom and I went in with her and sat on the edge of the tub. She was "bullshit" as they say in Boston because the doctor wouldn't tell her anything. She had to read it on the chart for herself. When she asked him what the nature of the problem was, he told her that it was a slight irregularity. Nothing more. He took a second pap smear, then he examined her through a speculum with a microscope.

Then he took two biopsy samples. She reconstructed what she'd overheard between the doctor and the nurse and what she'd read on the chart to arrive at this. Fortunately, she was able to read most of the medical abbreviations, CA for cancer, BX for biopsy. She hasn't really slept today. She's been angry, extremely angry, and is directing it at the doctor. And he's a worthy target.

I told her that whatever happened, I would always be right there with her. She said she wanted to be here, too. I wish I could mean what I said to the extent that I could literally be with her whatever happened, even the worst. But my metaphysical development hasn't taken me that far.

What happens now? The results of the biopsy. Can that really go either way? And if it's positive, then the hysterectomy? And will that be the end of it? Will my sweetheart then be safe? She has to wait three weeks to find out the results and said that she will somehow have to manage to put it out of her mind.

No one has ever died on me before. An uncle I wasn't close to when I was a boy. My grandfather who I wasn't close to because I didn't speak French. Same with the other one who I only saw once in my life. And a grandmother I saw only once, also. Wasn't there more than a language barrier between me and my grandparents, considering I seldom got to see them?

Three are dead, and they didn't "die on me" because I didn't know them. I have not yet grieved for the death of a loved one, and have never really thought about it, for I have never had a loved one before. But now I find the thought fearsome, and there is little that I fear that does not relate to Rebecca.

Has she, I now wonder, come into my life to satisfy several of my deficiencies? Love, selflessness, abandonment of my power and ego, so many gifts. Must grief be added to this list? Must it?

This too is attributable to the horrible Mr. Hyde, the schizoid sub-human aspect of her father. Yes, he has to be schizophrenic with at least those two fully distinct splits for how else could he ever have convinced Rebecca's mother of his innocence? How else could her mother believe that Rebecca was merely suffering from delusions? How else could Rebecca have learned about separate personalities at such an early age except with a resident teacher?

The bitter irony is that it can make him forgivable when all of my impulses otherwise want to destroy him slowly and painfully.

Rebecca has gone back to bed and I am sitting here writing these things, conscious of the fact that I am writing a book. My readers are wondering, what will happen to Rebecca? As I wonder. Will they wonder about me? Am I a "sympathetic character" in this book? Or do I think of myself too much as I am doing now?

I have concluded something astonishing, and here is how. It was by encountering the idea and seeing it cover the entire field of my knowledge and provide it with a unity and clarity that grandiosely overwhelms the character of the knowledge held previously. It is the sensation of having encountered pure truth.

I have concluded that Rebecca routinely and frequently has sexual escapades with other men, virtually whenever the opportunity presents itself. She is a slut, unbeknown to herself, for every such incident is immediately blocked from her memory. Lingering traces, rare recall episodes, and events resulting circumstantially from escapades have given us a wealth of clues, which have all fallen into place in the matrix of her repressed behavioral episodes.

Over the past few weeks, Rebecca has been struggling with what she described as something difficult coming out. Last weekend, she remembered that my brother raped her while we were there on our honeymoon. She was remembering it as she told me. I took it with equanimity.

The discovery of more immediate significance is the revelation that she continues to block out impermissible sexual experiences. It seems reasonable to assume that it is more than a single incident, but that, if the mechanism is alive and healthy, it is taking all of the exercise it can find opportunity for. The assumption is that she has a strong drive for this kind of ball-busting behavior, punishing men by showing them what she won't give to them again.

It was with this new concept that I was able to place dozens and dozens of miscellaneous events that I had otherwise found ways of dismissing, her pregnancy last November being not among the least of these.

There was the phone call from Joe, who, when told that Rebecca didn't know any Joe, told me that that was funny, she sucked his cock yesterday. There was her love for John the psychologist, who was unexplainably upset and sad when he learned she really was getting married. There was the night guard whose involvement with another woman at the hospital resulted in unexplainable stares of hatred from her. There were her references to Diane's affair with Dr. Lief, how it was sad to see it breaking up, how it had been understandable, as if stage-setting for what must be an affair with him of her own. There are the men who stare at her intensely when we walk. I don't even recall at the moment so many others that have occurred to me and which fit.

My wife is a slut. That is a curious situation to find myself in. My reaction is sexual excitement, only because my sex drive responds first. My mind can suddenly see pictures of Rebecca's mind, and that is where I get the reaction of excitement, of hope, and of encouragement because it is clear what must be done. There is a landscape littered with packets, each containing a repressed memory. None is aware of the other; and this is a problem in trying to satisfy that ball-busting sex drive, because each incident seems to be the first, rather than there being a summing up of previous experiences which would eventually lead toward satisfying that appetite. An early goal is to create connections between episodes so that there can be some sense of fulfillment of that drive.

A second early goal is to develop in her the habit of reminding herself that it is time to give herself permission for doing what she has done, in view of the fact that it is done and repressing it won't change that at all, prior to drawing down the curtain of repression. She needs to do this until she reaches the point where she is able to give herself permission for the least wrong of her activities; I trust that she will, at that point, remember episodes of similar intensity. Thus, she begins at the mildest end of the spectrum and proceeds at her own speed.

In the meantime, I am gravely concerned for her safety. She is apparently ball-busting numbers of men, and someday one of them will rape her and beat her, and she will come home saying she has been mugged. I have advised her that instead of endangering herself by refusing men who want more, she can also ball-bust by charging them, and that would probably avoid any hostile behavior from men. I told her to bring the money home and tell me the stories.

I have done my best to assure her that I accept her and will continue to do so, that even her most sluttish behavior will be seen by me as the symptom of a problem, not as culpable behavior. I think that I am holding up my strength while I attempt to teach Rebecca the new basic skills she must have, and that

I will then collapse.

Very interesting. I am very much taken with the idea of Rebecca being a hooker. It is sexually stimulating for me. I've read of such feelings, but didn't think they could be real.

There may have been an incident yesterday. Rebecca was depressed and cried in bed. She kept talking about her pregnancy, and of things related to having babies. I checked her genital area because she was complaining of internal pains, but all appeared normal. However, her vagina appeared clean and odorless, which suggested a very recent cleansing

She told about a gas company man having been in the foyer, and said she watched him through the peephole, that he was asking for the key to the penthouse apartment (there is none). Yesterday would have been her first chance. She got very sick with flu and missed work. But the night before, she was standing in front of her make-up mirror, and her face was joyous as she told me she would begin wearing her hair down when she went to work. She clearly was itching to get into action.

She went to get her paycheck yesterday, went to her bank, to Osco's. She put several dollars worth of quarters in the change can (for laundry, she said) as well as two dollar bills in my plastic coin box, an unprecedented action. This may have been "bringing home the money." But...quarters?

She seldom misses an opportunity to explain how carefully she shops and how much she is able to buy for very little money. This may be to dispel (or deny) any possible thought that she may have a "second source" of income.

If she did the burglary, it must have been as a diversion from whatever terrible thing happened at work or on her way home that day. She must have felt in the pits and needed an excuse for feeling that way in front of me. She never commented much on the loss of the computer. Possibly more denial there.

Tonight, I met her at work. She was high and mighty, nobody was good enough for her. Turns out she had been stung by the sudden switch in attitude toward her from her co-workers. Then she tells me how she recollected that, on her way out of work last Tuesday, there was something with the black guard. Like he was harassing her, and she really let him have it. But she doesn't know the words. Several men at work hung their heads away from her today.

She didn't comment on how she withstood the day physically after having been so ill, until asked, and then she let it drop. It had apparently not been a problem for her.

Tonight she smelled and tasted fresh, after a day's work in pantyhose. It is difficult to know what the clues are, but such as these are possibilities.

If she did the burglary, she could have been venting herself at the computer which had been taking much of my time away from her. It would have been a logical transference. And how could she open her own present, the one undisturbed item on my desk?

Yesterday, she had a slight numbness in her thighs. In the afternoon, it was also evident in her solar plexus. Today it has eased somewhat.

She said she was sore from last night (intercourse twice with me), when I touched her.

I feel that I can finally see through all of her behaviors, and understand what is underneath, what is going on. The delay in accomplishing this has come from being unable (unwilling) to imagine the proportions involved in her behavior.

Yesterday was the day after being violently ill, and it was her day off. But she was up and dressed in the morning, and awakened me for breakfast and saw me off to work.

Yesterday when I came home, Rebecca had just gotten home, an hour later than usual, and was still in her uniform. I very seldom see that. Usually, she changes into casual clothes or a bathrobe. She kept her uniform on for such a long time that I commented on it. She said that it would signal that she had to begin doing the dishes. "You're not home yet," I interpreted.

She was quiet, not very communicative. Came to me at my desk several times but didn't say anything serious or heavy. She was acting tired, drained. She said almost nothing at all about her day at work, when usually she has at least a half hour of tales to tell.

What tipped me off? I don't remember the thought processes. But I began to probe. I asked her about her errands she had run after work and didn't pick up anything unusual there. I pointed out that she hadn't yet said much about her day, and she impatiently

41

launched into explaining that she was upset because she wanted a baby, and she can't even have a kitten, and that seeing Donna's baby on Monday had upset her.

I asked her to remember earlier in the day, since this had occurred at work near the end of her shift. (I had to ask for that.) She said that it had been an easy day, that when she had finished up her work, she pitched in and helped some of the others finish. I asked her who she helped. She detailed how she helped, I think, Kay. I asked her who she helped next, and she got exasperated and said, "I don't know!"

It is quite unusual when Rebecca doesn't remember something in detail, especially something that occurred just earlier the same day. I suggested to her that she was blocking out who she helped next. I asked her what was the next thing she could remember, and it was being in the lounge, telling the above story about wanting a baby. She didn't remember getting there. That could mean that as much as an hour has been repressed.

I am doing my best mentally to keep track of signals or symptoms that indicate that something is currently in the process of being repressed. I have failed to persuade myself to keep written notes, and I know I will regret it.

Fatigue is such a symptom. Lack of interest in sex. So tight that it is not possible to penetrate her fully enough for intercourse. A certain amount of withdrawal and apparent depression. And curious occasional items such as delaying taking her uniform off, as if needing it for a cloak of some sort. No smiles, no loving hugs, although there are needy hugs.

I have been handling this drama quite well, largely by

staying high (and therefore wise). But today, the mysterious incident of yesterday, and the whole phenomenon, is starting to bother me. I shared a summary of it with Susan this afternoon. I needed to share it with someone and I can trust her. Her reaction breaks down like this: for the first three-fourths of the conversation, she merely didn't believe it. For the last quarter, she a) believed it, and b) was in amazement at herself for being capable of believing it.

Rebecca has her period this week. One day, she flowed very heavily, including clots the size of quarters and nickels. Her first association was with a miscarriage three years ago. Her suspicion is that this was a miscarriage. After a pause her next comment concerned her appointment to get birth control pills.

I said that she had been living with this new idea about herself for a little while now. I asked her how she was feeling about it. She said that she still didn't believe it, that she wanted proof. I shared ideas I have been having about some surveillance devices and asked if it would be okay with her if I implemented some of them in pursuit of proof. I asked several times before getting her clear approval, although it seemed completely sincere.

I am supposed to be grocery shopping now, but I can't bring myself to do it. I am feeling anxious. Rebecca is at therapy and will be home at 6:30. These are very heavy days in therapy.

I have been a lame duck for weeks now, at work. Awaiting my new contract. Shared my impatience with the commissioner on the elevator, and he excused it by saying, "That's the bureaucratic system."

Oh, my darling Rebecca. If only you could enjoy it! If only it didn't turn you into a wrung-out sponge. Whatever that behavior is all about, couldn't it somehow be okay all the way around? My love for you is incredible to me. I have taken you fully into my bosom, for I am not repelled by your problems, for they are as my own. The person you are is a vivid aspect of the person I am. You are more a part of me than my blood relatives, more than many of my own ideas of myself.

I am anxious and the pot is somewhat sedating, but I am still shifting back into anxiety here and there. I mean, what is this shit? It's happening right in front of my nose—I'm watching it happen! And I really have to stretch myself to be understanding and accepting of it. I barely make it, although I do seem to make it. But am I making it today, right now? I'm starting to crumble. Rebecca, part of me wants to just suppress you out of my mind. When I'm not with you, just forget you exist. That would be an easier way of dealing with it. But most of me recognizes you as part of myself, and is directed to being as helpful and nurturing to you as I can. The trouble right now seems to be that the lesser part of me wants its turn.

It's bad enough when a man has to be suspicious of his wife's behavior. But when we both have to be suspicious, isn't that a bit excessive? Give me a break.

I've been in a daze for perhaps a week. Perhaps as I write I will remember what it began with. It was learning that there had been some specific repressed incident that day. It was the first tape recording, but what I don't remember is what triggered me to buy that equipment. Somehow, we learned that she was repressing currently.

I had to reread the other file which has the account of lost time at the hospital followed by symptoms of repression in action. I didn't remember it—I had to read it all. I am writing honestly, uninhibited. I am high.

Am I cutting off my past that close to the bud? If I am dropping my past virtually as it emerges, how do I go about laying claim to it, all of it?

So I bought a voice-activated tape recorder and planted it. Not too cleverly, but enough so that she could find it only by looking for it. I "rehearsed" for a few days, listening to our ordinary sounds of living, learning to identify them. The real test would be, of course, Rebecca's next day off. That was last Tuesday.

I was listening to the tape at my desk, and when she came to me, she showed no curiosity whatever over the tape recorder, nor did she ask what I was listening to. Later, she asked, did I make a recording. I had not said anything aloud about the tape. She wanted to hear it. I had only just heard it once. I put it on the loud speakers and everything sounded normal. We were both pleased. But then I did a detailed analysis of the tape, and learned that the kitchen door had been opened to admit a youth or woman, that the porch door had been closed, that a man's voice said "I liked it." I tasted condom lubricant on her that night.

She was watching me do the last of the analysis. I began trembling, and said, my god, now I really do believe it. I went hyper. Rapid pulse, dazed, although I recognize that only now, tightly-controlled easy-going behavior. That daze just ended, ten o'clock tonight. I smoked up. Just had the most incredible sex.

She followed suit, stayed controlled. Off and on all evening, we would speculate about details. She would get impressions, like it was the kitchen door. Like she was thinking that I would never find out. We both came home sick the next day, and met at home at noon. It was exactly the correct surprise, because we consoled and comforted each other until we were feeling completely merged into each other, and we made wonderful love together. We were healed. Or so it seemed.

Wednesday was uneventful. Today is Thursday. Eventful. She took today off as a personal day for an appointment with a gynecologist, following my early advice that she have a pap smear and examination, and get on the pill. (I also supplied her with condoms, none of which has been used so far.)

That appointment was this morning, and she met me at the office for lunch. She asked if she could spend some time at my desk before leaving for home, and she read the paper while I word processed. She got home somewhere between 2:30 and 3:00, and had to leave for a 4:15 therapy appointment.

Dr. B (or someone) had called to make the appointment earlier because of a meeting conflict, Rebecca had told me at the time. When she returned from therapy today, she had gone overtime fifteen minutes, she said. I had the tape on the loudspeakers when she came home, with the volume up high, trying to hear a voice. Rebecca's voice, saying something like, 'Just sit right here, Ben.'

Astonished, she said, "Wha-a-at?" She insisted on listening to the whole tape, and I asked her to wait until I had analyzed it. We listened to it together, using my rough analysis, a list of sound descriptions numbered according to the tape counter. We did our best to reassure each other. And though we imagined the "worst," we weren't prepared for what a detailed analysis revealed for the segment surrounding the voice.

"Ben" had brought cocaine. Rebecca had been feeling bright-eyed and energetic, and suddenly it made sense to her. She had been upset last night thinking about her gyn exam, fearful, as always, of what terrible thing might be found. And therapy, where she gave a rapid and vivid summary of our recent events. Dr. B's first exposure to the idea of Rebecca's multiple personalities, so Rebecca affirms.

After a day like that, she should be dragging her ass two feet behind her. But here she is, pestering me to fix supper because she is hungry. Hyper. It fits. She didn't call it an impression. She said, "I can imagine running into some old friend from Mass. Mental and having him in briefly to do a snort of cocaine; I think that's all it was."

But she did have an impression, that of running into a woman she might have known in the past and inviting her in for tea, spinning her web that way, as the spider said to the fly in the children's story, my god, I've got to check out what she remembers about that story. She could be using it as an archetype for her behavior. We do judge that she is usually an adolescent in this other split, which may not be too old to remain influenced by a children's story.

Tuesday, the detailed analysis showed that the tape recorder had been turned off and rewound some amount during the time Rebecca was home. The same seems evident about today's tape, although I haven't finished analyzing it yet. Thank god she has a limited number of days off! Not that her split is not active at every opportunity, but that a day off offers abundant opportunities, irresistible opportunities, for the split. It seems to be a sure bet that some clues will be taped on every day off.

We have recognized it as a battle of wits. Tuesday, we thought it was miraculous that we had taped some clues on the very first attempt. Today, it seems inevitable.

I haven't explained that we soon agreed to collaborate openly in pursuit of concrete evidence of the split, recognizing that Rebecca was a double-agent. I work on the assumption that I am unable to hide anything from her. On that basis, I am supposed to outwit her. Yes, me. Rebecca is anxious to see it happen, and scared to death, too.

Yesterday, we went walking on an errand. First, two teenage boys headed toward us, and divided to go around us. The curly-headed one on Rebecca's side stared intently at her all the way past. We had seen him a few weeks ago with a couple of other boys on the sidewalk, and he'd called to us, "Isn't love wonderful?" I think he's one of them.

Only five minutes later, we passed Janet who was with two other women. She gave Rebecca a very warm greeting, followed by a wistful expression. I had never heard of Janet, but she works as an OT with Rebecca. Rebecca revealed an ongoing lesbian relationship with Janet.

When we returned home, I asked about my boss,

48

Mitch. It seems that the feelings between Becky and Mitch arc quite intense and involved at this point. Mitch is giving me money at work. Friday, the tape recorder had been shut off, and there was an extra door opening and closing on it, in spite of the fact that Rebecca had only 45 minutes until I came home.

She revealed the extent of her lesbian relationship with Jackie, which apparently involved only one full sexual experience, still repressed but with evidence in the morning (a year or two ago) and a lesser experience at Ashford House, but apparently there were and may still be very strong feelings there, a certain real intimacy.

It is a lot to deal with. My rapid pulse is less intense with each revelation, however. I feel stretched to my capacity, but still on top of it.

She has a good aptitude for electronics. She figured out all the switches and features of the stereo with only a few questions or hints from me. She has apparently figured out how the tape recorder works in enough detail to know about rewinding and recording over material she wants erased. Clue: if the radio is on, it is on to use up the tape that needs to be recorded over. But that applies only to the first time. Since, she has turned off the tape recorder altogether, and either muffled the microphone or switched the voice activation to its low setting. She catches on too fast for me. Or she has someone helping her. The others.

Today, we are preparing Cornish hens as a birthday dinner for Rebecca. My heart is not in it. I am preoccupied to the max. We plan to walk along the Charles after dinner. She has been housecleaning today, and I have been plotting. I don't need more evidence for myself; but I need to know that this is really happening in the objective world. I need it to be consensual information. My proofs so far, on tape, are not completely irrefutable. Someone could refuse to interpret them as I have. And I know that I am going to get a clear, untampered tape, soon. And I am frightened at the prospect of listening to it. It's going to shock the shit out of both of us.

I am feeling very anxious. My breathing is shallow for hours at a time. I get welling feelings for a deep breath, and I take one, deliberately, just to get more air. I smoke up, have a beer, keep trying to shift my perspective to a safe place. It occurred to me that my initial reaction to learning of Becky's episodes, which was that it was salacious material, was at the time the easiest perspective for dealing with it. I couldn't deal with it at all any other way. To my credit, a good part of me also accepted this as a problem of my own, because I considered Rebecca to be a part of my own self. I cannot muster up much interest today in the salacious aspects of the lives and loves of Becky et al. I am suffering now, along with Rebecca, tormented by the unknown, terrified of what the outcome of all of these revelations might be.

We got married on Christmas day, and it was the most blissful day I can remember having. Then, three months passed. I'm trying to remember what it was like for those three months, before she told me about sleeping with my brother during our honeymoon.

She was usually dead tired, and went to bed at 8:00. She was often exhausted on the sofa when I came home. Sometimes, she was up and dressed, feeling chipper. But most of the time she was exhausted. We quarreled about it, because I complained that if her job was taking that much out of her, it was too much, because it wasn't leaving enough of her for me.

She believed that she was pregnant in January. For three or four days, she embraced the idea, talking about taking special care of her health, and on and on. As if she didn't remember that I'd had a vasectomy.

When I asked by whom she might be pregnant, she said, "Why, you, of course!" When I asked how, she said something must have reversed itself in me and allowed sperm to come through. I finally got her to let go of this fantasy.

Various times after that, she talked of her pregnancy with Seth, about Donna at work having a baby, about having a miscarriage, about us having a baby. It was a recurrent theme with her. I also pointed out to her that she couldn't consider having a baby as long as her energy level was so low that she couldn't make it through the day without collapsing, because a baby requires energy 24 hours a day.

I busied myself setting up an enterprise that could develop into my source of support working at home. A lot of my attention went into it. I spent time researching telecomputers, figuring out where to get the money for one, and most evenings were spent at least partly at my desk. I was also intent on my campaign for a new job at DPH.

I'm sure she must have felt ignored, for I would leave her to do the dishes or her exercises while I worked at my desk. The usual schedule was this: I come home, say hello, go to my desk and read the mail, find other things to do, she does the dishes, I cook supper while she sleeps, wake her up and we eat, she cleans up for bed while I go back to my desk. I tuck her in, usually postponing sex to my bedtime a few hours later.

On the weekends that she didn't work, we did the laundry, the shopping, other errands, and she house cleaned while I did other things. When she worked the weekend, I got high, walked errands in the neighborhood, eyed the women, and put a lot of time into developing my business.

I began noticing other women more and more, until my fantasies began stepping into actions. Gradually, we lost our intimacy with each other. There were exceptional moments, but by and large our days and nights passed with little intimacy, and with occasional hard feelings.

There was little insight or revelation during those three months. We were taking our life together pretty much for granted and going with it. After all, it was winter, and we didn't think we were supposed to feel all sunshiny. We felt that we were gradually building our life together, setting up our future. I didn't give a special amount of thought to the present. And I may be assuming too much by describing Rebecca's feelings as my own, for I didn't stay in touch with her feelings very well during this time.

A lot of those three months was spent thinking that Rebecca was my piece, my sex object, my fulfilled fantasy of a sex goddess of my own. I worried about thinking like that, and tried to steer myself away from it, but it attracted me right back. While we would make love, I would be saying to myself, fuck me, you whore, I own you, this is what you're good for, you are my living blow-up sex doll.

I have a handicap when it comes to spying on Rebecca. Because my memory fades out quickly, it takes me a long time to make connections, piece things together.

It's still a great gulp for me to realize that it was after a year and three months of living with Rebecca that I learned that her splits were currently very active and repressed, and then only because she told me.

I passed up many clues because I didn't realize that I needed clues for anything happening now. We explained away her pregnancy in November. The test was wrong. We explained away her exhaustion. She was just dealing with too much. True, as it turns out, but with much more than we realized.

She was not careless during our first year, however. I never tasted condom on her, never noticed anything out of order. She kept immaculate house, with everything always under control that way, a good way of dealing with any clues that might be present. It didn't occur to me not to trust her, and I didn't look for suspicious things. I accepted her easy explanations, which were usually clever enough to hold true on their own.

Now, she is leaving me clues. Perhaps they are the very same clues, but now I am observing them as such. One time last year, she told me that it depressed her to come home to the house with dishes on the table and the bed not made. I didn't question that at the time, but it strikes me now as a curious statement. I think she straightens up the house before inviting people in, and this was cutting into that small amount of time between the time she gets home from work and the time I get home.

She told me this morning that she was up three times during the night to go to the bathroom, that she was very tired. But the tape recorder had apparently been turned off because it didn't record any bathroom sounds, and it did record the front door opening sometime between bedtime and the time Rebecca turned the radio on, which I think was 4:30, the time she usually gets up (although she doesn't ordinarily turn the radio on that early).

Except on her weekends off, she is inevitably up before I am in the morning. She always awakens me, never the other way around. I sleep like a log, never noticing her getting up in the night, nor anything else for that matter. I am thinking that she is up most of the night in other splits. It's incredible to me to suspect such a thing, but she was exhausted this morning, and we went to bed early. Everything is suspect.

I am looking forward to knowing a lot more than I do, because when everything is suspect, there is little left to provide grounds for intimacy with my beloved. If all of my suspicions are true, then she is one of the most physically enduring and energetic people ever. I don't think anyone could live such a life on purpose.

It is a strange life I am leading these days. I am filled with constant panic, which I constantly struggle to hold in check. I can't easily focus on my work. It's a good thing that I am in a hiatus between jobs, because if I had a heavy load to handle right now, I'd have to just walk away from it.

My thinking is very little on the future these days. I am consumed with the search for knowledge and understanding of what is going on, consumed with the anxiety that the present must be changed, that this cannot go on, that we have no future until this is resolved. Only a future of todays, today again, day after day.

My mind certainly gets into a muck! I've been desperate, and in my desperation have been trying to fight those others in her head-on, but she takes the brunt of it. I am just now realizing that I cannot fight them that way; my route is to fight them by strengthening Rebecca. I must entrust her portion of the battle to her and not try to spare her from it, which I could not anyway. I can only strengthen her as much as I can.

I think that when I told her of propositioning Francoise, she was so angered that the others came alive, much more so than they had been. I think it was the very next day that she came home with the clues that something had happened at work that day. It was enough to pique my curiosity, enough to tell me that something had indeed happened, but not enough to get her into trouble. No specifics, just the general framework of paranoia.

And since then, it has been almost daily that enough clues have been given to me (I thought by my cleverness and her errors, but perhaps more the other way around) to set my heart racing, my mind panicking, my lungs gulping for air. I haven't been smoking much pot the last several days. I am running low, but mainly I was too depressed to remember what it can do. Or perhaps it can do it only when that thought comes to mind.

She (they) has been attempting to destroy me and destroy our marriage, and it appears that the design is to push me into being the guilty party. All of this just to punish me for spending an hour with Francoise.

Please, dear, enough is enough.

My only tactic at this point seems to be to return to that blissful state that is the real me and Rebecca, and nurture it for all I'm worth. I must now face the sacrifice of the remnants of my attraction to other women. I have made some rapid progress here to date, having had many days when I was not overtly signaling to women I desired. And days when they were the farthest thing from my mind.

Of course, I have been distracted, extremely so, and I must smoke more pot more regularly so that I can have a better grip on this perspective that loving Rebecca is the only answer. So, now the remnants go. I will permit myself to admire pretty women, and I will reroute most of the sexual attraction to more appropriate things.

Today is Saturday and I am home alone. Rebecca is working. I am trying to get my head straight; I have not smoked today. Most of the coping mechanisms that occur to me involve striking out at Rebecca. I am not fully sold on the multiple personality bit because I have observed too many "transitions" that showed me that her mind contained both the errant Rebecca as well as my Rebecca.

She expressed some upset last night about her condition, saying, "How do you think it feels to be unable to live a normal life?" But generally speaking, she is not at all upset that I can see. We have estimated that 10% of her loves me and 90% of her plays me for a sucker. That 90% just plain hates me.

And she thinks I'm supposed to accept that just because she is unaware of it.

My current thinking about her condition is that she has denial down pat, and walks open-eyed into her escapades, trusting her ability to deny the whole thing right out of her memory. I base this partly on the fact that she calls me at work to find out if I am there, to clear some time for herself. She remembers those phone calls and lays claim to them. But she acts as if she is unaware of the real purpose of the calls. She is not very willing to be suspicious of her own behavior, and I think it is because it is too important to her; she wants her problems; they fulfill her somehow; she does not seem intent, at least not often, on really getting them resolved.

She is complacent about them; they aren't all that bad to her. I'm supposed to be complacent, too, she thinks. I'm supposed to just tell myself that it isn't really her doing all of those things, and ignore the consequences of her rampant sucking and fucking.

I can't ignore it. Everyone in the building has probably had sex with her, and I'm supposed to ignore that. Half the people we walk by on the sidewalk have probably had sex with her; I'm supposed to ignore their stares, their whistles, their facial expressions. Somehow, I'm just supposed to say to myself, well, that's not really my wife out there pushing her pussy. It's just her body, her voice, her shell.

I don't like knowing that my apartment is visited by strangers several times every day and night. I am angry once again about the burglary because I feel certain that it happened because of her behaviors.

She is destroying me. I have come home from work after half an hour for the past three days, unable to work. I can't stop thinking about it; it consumes me.

So how do I come up with a satisfactory way of coping with this fucked up mess? Part of me keeps screaming, get the hell out of it before it sucks you completely dry, and there's not enough of you left to live your life. Get out while you still can. But another part of me loves my Rebecca dearly, and would never forgive itself for abandoning her. No one has ever stuck with her before, and I could be that important person to her.

Not so long ago, I didn't know about her voluminous fucking around. Ignorance was bliss. Now, I feel like a champion sucker, a fool. She tells people at work what a wonderful husband I am, and they say, where did you find a man like that? But I can hear them thinking, where did you find such a super sucker, when you are such a slut?

If I stick with her for the long haul recovery, which may be many years, what will I have? Possibly I will still have the most precious intimate relationship I have ever had, preserved somehow. Possibly I will be dead.

Is this real life? I got so bored with real life as I knew it that I got divorced and went exploring. What I found was Rebecca, and we have not had a real life together. And lately it has become so totally unreal, so misfit, so distorted and perverted, so filled with anguish and anxiety, that I cannot even figure out how to cope with it.

Part of me says that this is the suffering I have inflicted on others, coming back to haunt me. Karma. Part of me says that I will continue living with her but will stop being a sucker, at least as far as household chores and expenses are concerned; but that is striking out. But maybe there's something in it anyway; maybe it would help me feel better.

I "hung" the gremlin doll by the neck from the light cord in my closet. Striking out. But better the gremlin than me. I am not really suicidal, I don't think.

I have a whole day off and I can't think of a single thing I would like to do just for me. I have no friends these days; she has cut me off from everyone; she has me isolated so that she can control me better. I wouldn't mind if things were more normal, but I feel so alone without friends. There is simply no one I can call or write about this. Perhaps Joe. He'd love it, and be sympathetic at the same time. But what does that get me? I need to cope with it, not just talk about it.

It has been ages since any of my friends has responded to my correspondence. I suspect that she has scared them all off, unknown to me. I'm thinking of writing to them and asking. But if it turns out to be true, then what do I do with my anger?

The tape recordings I have been making in the apartment while I'm gone haven't yielded much of anything lately; I didn't make any after her birthday party because I just wouldn't have been able to tolerate the thought that after that wonderful celebration she got up in the night and sucked somebody off.

I met her at work on Wednesday, and it was clear from Catherine's face that they had intended a rendezvous after work. I met her after work the next two days, also, just to use up that time period for her. But then I gave up on that tactic, too, because I simply cannot stop her. She'll suck a nigger's dick at work. She'll leave the floor, leave the hospital long enough to come home and fuck. Shell suck somebody off in the back seat of a car on her way home. I can't stop it. How do I deal with that?

I can't stand to listen to more tapes, but I will have to. I'm supposed to just draw a line in my mind that divides my Rebecca from the others. Just like that. I'm supposed to "realize" that it isn't really her. The problem is that it is 90% of her; I'm supposed to ignore 90% of her? Just because she doesn't or can't lay claim to 90% of herself? Sure.

So what do I do? If I lose her, I will have lost the greatest love of my life, and I can't feel at all certain that I will ever find something like that again. I'm willing to pay the prices of keeping our relationship together; the problem is that I don't know how to do it. I'm broke, emotionally, rationally, socially.

The only thing that helps at all is smoking pot; that wipes away my ego-involvement with the world out there, and leaves me feeling peaceful. And wise. And long-suffering. But lately even that hasn't been working as well. I come down quickly and become angry, hostile. I really, with all of my heart, want to destroy those others in her. But I can't get at them. She is cleverer than I am, has more savvy. She is formidable. She'll do exactly as she pleases for as long as she likes. I can't stop her.

I try to make her want to stop, but only seldom does she seem interested or concerned. The rest of the time, she seems to want to preserve the problem behavior intact.

Part of our problem currently is that I do not fully accept the multiple personality idea. Maybe there is some of that there, but damn it, she seems to walk right into her escapades without a shift. I just can't trust it. I think it's mostly expert denial, which she treats like a secret power, and protects it as such.

I don't know what to do today. She has become my whole life. I am lost without her. I hate 90% of her so bad it makes me want to vomit with disgust, and I love 10% of her more intensely than I have ever loved anyone before. How do I draw a separating line between these two?

If she were merely an embarrassment to me, that I could deal with, I think. It's a whole hell of a lot more than that. It's partly my ego, as she pointed out when I told her that she, the totality of her, did not fulfill my image of what a wife was supposed to be.

My wife is not supposed to be doing so much outside sucking and fucking that she is too tired for me. Or any at all for that matter. Yes, it offends my ego, my sense of how life ought to be lived. She calls that wrong; I don't see why my ego shouldn't be completely offended.

She sees it as a side-issue, something I should be able to just put into check. I asked her how she would feel if I fucked five women every day, then came home too tired for her. She admitted she wouldn't like it.

She denies any sense of responsibility for the behaviors of the others, claims they are totally independent of her. They are not; they are all mixed up into each other and into the 10% Rebecca. They are all there; she has said she can exert a restraining influence over them. But unless I badger her about it a great deal, she seems not to consider the possibility of actually restraining them.

She is just plain having fun, at my expense, by not doing everything she can to restrain the others, by not being truly interested in restraining them. She seems to be heavily invested in the others, and unwilling to try to eradicate them or integrate them or anything.

She shows so little interest in defying them that I suspect the little interest she does show is lip service to pacify me.

They are her friends. They control her, perhaps. Yes, they control her, probably. She is just as defenseless against them as I am. Or so she must feel. But I know that she could defy them, if only she could muster up enough conviction about it.

That is what sticks in my throat. She wants the tapes, but she recognizes how much they make me suffer. She is not dedicated to solving her problems. That's what disturbs me the most. She's content to think that they will continue for perhaps several more years. It's like saying, let's not rush things. I'm having fun. Like saying, well, you've put up with it for this long, what's the matter with you now? Well, now I know. That's what's the matter. Now it's part of my own personal reality. I'm not objective about it anymore, I'm involved. Two ways: as a lover, and as a sucker and a fool.

Yesterday morning, I listened to the overnight tape enough to hear a conversation at the front door. It was no better quality than the other tapes so far, but it included phrases like "brush your teeth and take a shower," and "tell George when he's working..." and "...tell me I'm heading all over, and that's a lie!" and "Poor George, what's he going to say to me when he finds out it's guys like that?" and a male voice saying "You gotta kill some pain." It was Mary next door. I didn't really recognize Rebecca's voice, but I left for work believing that Rebecca had gone to Mary's during the night, I supposed to have sex with her.

We listened to the tape together when I got home. There was also a man's voice, and he was called Joe in one sentence. There was reference to $35. Rebecca's reaction to the tape was like my reaction to the first tape—she was finally struck with the truth, and showed a panicky resolve to fight the problem.

She interpreted the tape to mean that Mary was lining up Johns for her. Rebecca said my towel was damp in the morning when she showered. She said she reached for it, found it was damp, then said to herself, "Why am I reaching for that towel—it's George's."

She had the impression that when she got up to go to the bathroom, she returned to bed, but then went to the sofa and dozed, waiting for Mary's knock on the door. She handled a difficult day's work very professionally, and believes she was on speed, and that she took more at noon. She doesn't know where the money is. She thinks that Mary may be paying her some other way—drugs, or "protection," which she couldn't define. Or she thinks maybe Mary is holding her money in escrow.

We need Mary, or at least could use her, to tell us about the behavior of this counterpart.

A few months ago, Rebecca arranged for us to visit with Mary one evening. During that visit, Mary was wide-eyed with apparent apprehension, looking like she couldn't figure us out. She told that she had been a high-priced call girl. She now has at least one girlfriend staying with her part-time, so Linda told me at the laundromat Saturday. We haven't seen Mike, her boyfriend, for many weeks now.

I slept on the floor in front of the front door last night

to prevent it from opening in the night. As usual, I slept soundly and heard nothing in the night.

I had an attack at the table during supper. I tried eating my hot dog sandwich and suddenly felt nauseous and confined. I began breathing desperately, tore my clothes off, and let my knees swing sideways to comfort myself. It lasted about five minutes. Rebecca tried to touch me, but it took my breath away. I had to turn on the window fan to cool down. She took my pulse—92, high for me.

During sex, I ejaculated weakly without a climax. This morning, I am still having difficulty breathing and my heart is fast.

I haven't eaten much in the past two weeks, and have lost about 15 pounds.

I gave Mitch an opportunity to talk yesterday. I said, I haven't shared this with you before, but my wife is seriously mentally ill, and people are taking advantage of her, including someone I consider a close friend. He choked on his pipe, put it aside, shuffled some papers, then said, "Hey, is it the guy who was at the party (Gus)?" I said it's hard to know who to rule out. A bit later, he faced me square on and said, "Well, there's nothing I can do to help you out, is there?" I left it at that for now. He loves danger, and I may have only added some spice to his affair with Rebecca. He starts vacation today. I warned Rebecca—she has today off. He needs his balls busted real bad.

The motion sensor apparently hasn't stopped nighttime activity for Mrs. Hyde et al. I figured out this morning that by walking along the wall, it was possible to reach the unit and shut it off without triggering it. Rebecca has been very tired the past few mornings—very grouchy yesterday—and this morning my towel was wet again.

I went with her to therapy yesterday and shared some of what I've been going through, plus details on Sunday night's tape, the one with a conversation at the front door. During the remainder of the session, I waited outside while Dr. B talked with four of the others, Rebecca told me, 4-, 8-, and 10-year olds, and Mrs. Hyde.

I didn't make tapes last night. I am getting bogged down with the labor of transcribing them. The previous two nights I put a recorder on the night stand and it was turned off both nights, and turned back on in time to catch the alarm clock going off. We agreed this morning that we will have to point the sensor at the bedroom door and sleep with the door closed. And put an alarm on the porch door.

It is such a battle of wits, a losing battle so far. I resolved this morning to assume a warrior stance—change my habits so that I don't sleep so soundly. I am quitting all smoking and drinking, will drink coffee in the evenings, will eat lightly, take nutritional supplements, and give myself suggestion. I need more time, also, and will attempt to get by on less sleep. I feel it is important to develop a business I can operate from home so I can have full control of my schedule, and so I can spend maximum time with Rebecca.

I took away Rebecca's keys to the apartment.

Yesterday at work, Susan asked me when I was going to get sick of it all. I realized that I am, have been, very sick of it. There's not much of it that I can do anything about, but I can preserve the privacy of the apartment, and protect the property in it. So I took away her keys this morning.

It brought out a series of the others. She threatened first to leave because she considered the idea intolerable; that was this morning. I told her that she was my wife and wasn't going anywhere. Then, she felt punished. There was some of that in there.

After listening to the Sunday night tape where she was at the door talking with Mary, she responded with the first display of determination to tackle her problems that I have seen from her.

Yesterday, I realized that I had been riding high on that display for a week, but that there hadn't been any more of it. It was a five-minute flash and that was all. She returned to her complacency, rolling merrily along.

Also, I sat in on the first half of her therapy session, and observed that Dr. B had not been told about my brother or about many other things, that Rebecca was not really being open in therapy at all. Our conversation this morning boiled down to the fact that I should butt out and leave everything to therapy.

I pointed out that she wasn't being honest and open in

therapy, and that at that rate it held little hope. So, yes, I was punishing her for not continuing her resolve to work at solving her problems. Today, we talked endlessly about it, with me repeating what I wanted over and over as if she had never heard me say it before. I was talking with several of the others, each in turn.

At the table tonight, she screamed and pounded her fists and ranted and raved. I laughed. She felt suicidal. I told her that there was also another choice, that of resolving to fight back, that even if she didn't know how to fight back, at least she could have the attitude of a fighter. More screaming.

The keys must be really important to the others, judging from the amount of attempted intimidation I witnessed. At this point, the others are not intimidating; at this point, I feel that if Rebecca cannot adopt a fighter's attitude, nothing is going to improve, and more merry rolling is not what I will settle for. I pushed her hard, explaining that I understood that she felt cornered, but that until she passes through the crisis of being cornered and choosing a direction—her choices seem to be suicide or fighting back—nothing is going to get any better, and that I was deliberately pushing her.

I told her that if she isn't going to show that she is interested in helping herself, she is not going to attract much help from others, including me. I really see my only choice as pushing her to change her attitude, to choose to fight.

It was an exceptionally dramatic display at the table tonight. She was furious. She decided that she had to lie down. I walked into the living room, and immediately out came my Rebecca asking for a hug, all gentle and soft and warm and loving. Just like that.

She discussed how she felt pushed out of her head by the others while at the table, and that her recollection of the conversation was spotty. We lay in bed for a while and talked, much more calmly. She fell asleep, and I came out to write this.

Upon calmer examination, the thing with the keys is a good idea, and she is thinking of spending her days off at day hospital in order to have a reasonably safe environment. She is planning to meet me at my office after work each day rather than spend an hour locked out, though I had offered to change my working hours to coincide with hers. She is also planning to spend her vacation at day hospital.

I discussed other possible ways that she could structure her days off, but she doesn't have enough confidence in herself to believe that she could successfully manage her days on her own.

I was so depressed by the time I got home yesterday that I just smoked and drank and got worse. She bitched me out off and on. By the time we went to bed, I didn't care about anything anymore. I didn't bother setting the motion sensor alarm last night. I didn't set up any tape recorders.

She had taken two Serax, and when I went to bed I asked her if she had taken anymore. She hadn't and I was disappointed. I told her that the sensor alarm wasn't set. I had to coax her into setting it herself. I told her that I didn't care anymore, that if she wanted it set, fine, she could set it, otherwise she could forget it.

I couldn't stay in bed. I got up and bedded down on the couch and tossed for two hours before finally falling asleep. In those two hours, I formulated the idea of taking away her keys.

It won't stop her; it will just stop her from using the apartment. I hope it doesn't force her into taking greater risks. Apparently, the apartment is seen as a safe place for her escapades. I am hoping very much that she is really that safety-conscious, that she will not take greater risks.

She saw the doctor last month and was given medication for PID. This month, exactly the same thing occurred. When the doctor asked (today) if she had multiple sex partners, she told her about her problem. That was remarkable.

My appetite returned after Rebecca responded to that Sunday night tape with determination to fight back. But it's been on again, off again, since then. Right now, I'm having an apple because I'm hungry, even after a good supper. I'm feeling rather successful about today; I don't know what really got accomplished, but I stood my ground against the others and even laughed in their faces, and that's something.

I didn't give in to her threat that she will leave me, and that's something because she has used that over and over again as a way of keeping me in line—off her back. Unless she simply decides not to come home one day, she can't move out without keys, and that's good. I don't have to pay attention to that threat any more.

She asked when she could get her keys back. I told her it would be when we mutually agreed that the risk of the others using the apartment was negligible. She asked how we would know when that time had come, and I told her I didn't know.

I talked with her at some length today about her constant habit of exaggerating everything she talks about. She defended it by saying that she felt she had to exaggerate things in order to get people to believe her. I told her that people recognize exaggeration as a kind of lie, and that they will not believe her anyway, that she needs to be responsible about the words that come out of her mouth, that she needs to speak accurately and honestly. I told her that I suspect she sees her problems as overwhelming because she exaggerates them to herself, that if she could stop doing that, the problems might appear more manageable.

By taking away the keys, I no longer have to make tapes. That relieves me of a lot of work, because I was spending about two hours every day listening to the damn things. I could have saved $500 by taking her keys away in the first place, for that is how much I have spent on recorders, phone taps, cassettes, etc. Microcassettes were running $100 a month, and I can't afford to keep that up.

But until I had the tapes, we didn't really know the dimensions of the problems, so I guess I couldn't have avoided the expense really. I wish I had thought to record our conversation at the table. I think I'll start using the recorders to tape some of our conversations. Conversation is too polite a word—arguments isn't really quite right either—I don't know what to call them. Hassles?

A few days before the last entry, I accompanied Rebecca to her therapy appointment. Dr. B talked to us afterward for a moment, telling me that my anger was going to put Rebecca back into the hospital, that I needed a "teaspoon of patience" with breakfast. It shocked me, and when we got home, we talked for a long time, probing. I led, with a number of specific questions.

We talked about how we drift into an absence of intimacy that cuts off communication between us. She said she drew down a curtain between us when things became difficult, that it was a defense. I asked her why she pulled that curtain down. She said she feared me because I am a man, that she feared men because they can rape her emotionally, as well as abuse her in other ways. I asked her to assess me as a man, and she felt that I was different. We agreed that it was important for her to reveal her real feelings to me in order to maintain the intimacy necessary for me to avoid danger. It was a very productive talk, and enabled me to be compassionate for almost a week.

Then something happened after about six days. I don't remember it at the moment, but it sent me into a depression.

Then she got out one night. She awakened with a pulled muscle in her lower neck, and told me later in the day that her waking impression was that she had injured herself while climbing off the porch during the night.

Rebecca said that at her last session, Dr. B seemed to renege on the whole situation, showed no willingness to believe any longer in the multiple personality, and refused to communicate with the therapist I have begun seeing. We decided it was time to seek a specialist. We arranged for one at Mass. General and he has seen Rebecca once so far; it went well.

I have had two sessions with my therapist so far. At the second, we talked about my reaction to love being taken away from me. I ended up, after the session, realizing that I have been deliberately and tenaciously clinging to an idea that's not true, that just because

Rebecca has these other behaviors does not mean that she doesn't love me. It has made a big difference for me. But the real important realization is that I was holding on to that idea, even in spite of occasional attempts to dismantle it. That is alarming to me.

It's difficult to face the fact that there are bondages in me like that, operating full steam with only a bit of my awareness. Bondages that may be preventing me from being the writer I want to be, from being in touch with my feelings, from managing my job or my businesses with clarity of the situation. Bondages that I don't remember forming, that if presented with a clear choice I would probably choose to destroy. Bondages that I may never discover.

Was my discovery of the bondage to associating my perceptions of not-so events to anger that I had lost love, was this discovery fortuitous?

My Dr. L is sharp, though, and pointed out (in only the second session!) that he saw some sort of triad between me and my love object and a third party whom I saw as interfering with the love I was receiving. He pointed it out; I considered it at the time; and later on I applied it to Rebecca, and it worked.

Perhaps there was an escape last night; our evidence is very slight: Rebecca's impression that there was a woman, her inability to ask me to go down on her this morning when we awakened and made love, her speculation that someone could have shut off the power to the apartment and told her through the bedroom window so that she could shut off the motion sensor and walk right out the front door, her generally being depressed and fearful when she awakened this morning, and some small fingernail marks on her thigh.

It could be that something happened, but while I admit that, I am not inclined to think so. I had a bondage before that forced me to think so in order to arouse my anger. This time, I didn't really have to do it, and I didn't. Are you angry, Rebecca asked me. No, I really wasn't at all; it hadn't occurred to me to be angry; I was only being thoughtful, wondering about the correlation between Rebecca awakening wrong and being out during the night.

I did chores all day long, including a mountain of dishes (about our maximum mountain, actually, since almost everything was dirty). I cooked dinner. Now, I am sitting on the back porch writing, and it is a little too cold to do this here for very long.

We have spent a week of vacation together. It had phases. The first phase was dealing with Rebecca's anxiety over her last appointment with Dr. B Friday afternoon, and Monday morning I made phone calls in search of a specialist. We agreed on the plan, although Rebecca would soon follow every agreement with some objection leading to changing to any therapist handy rather than seeking a specialist.

Monday and Tuesday were a phase of apprehension and wonder over the pending Wednesday appointment with the specialist, Dr. O. Then there was the phase of seeing psychiatrists. We saw the specialist on Wednesday (he saw her, not me, but I was there), and I had my session on Thursday.

Thursday night, Maggie and Paul came for dinner, which gave us a transition into our vacation proper. Friday, we took a picnic to Revere Beach and enjoyed eating on the rocks in the sun. It was a perfect day. We had the occasional company of a Basset hound, who was a delight to Rebecca.

Yesterday, we took the Provincetown I to Provincetown. We had thought that our day was going to emphasize being in Provincetown, but it turned out that we had six hours on the boat and only three in town. In those three, we walked from restaurant to restaurant, not believing the high prices we were reading on menus posted in the windows, certain that soon we would come across a restaurant with real prices, all the while jostling among a throng of tourists, seldom able to walk side by side.

Eventually, we gave in to the idea that lunch was going to cost us a fortune, so we decided on what we wanted. Fried clam dinner. We went into a pharmacy because the flint had run out in my lighter, and while there had the inspiration to ask where to find fried clams, since we had not yet seen it on any menus. The Lobster Pot, we were told, and off we went. Thirty dollars. Fried seafood platter. Sour cream apple crumb pie, really wonderful.

A few minutes walking along the shore, then back to the boat. We had found out on the way over that the boat wasn't any fun, so we didn't even try on the way back. We just found a booth and sat. For three hours. We were happy to get home last night. Today has been quiet, a day of rest. And that is our summer vacation.

I got word Wednesday that my contract has finally been signed and delivered. So I really do have a job to go to on Tuesday. Rebecca works tomorrow but I have the holiday because there would be no one at work to start me.

Tuesday is her first day off alone without keys. She plans to swim in the morning, meet me for lunch, and do some library work for me in the afternoon. I hope her other days work out as well.

Well, today I don't feel so good about it. Both towels were wet this morning and already in the laundry basket by the time I got to the bathroom. Rebecca was acting hang-dog guilty, and I was too asleep at breakfast to pick up on it. After she left for work, I went for a shower, found the towels gone, and checked them in the laundry basket. She was out last night.

The only way she can be getting out is for someone to shut off the power to the apartment from the basement long enough for her to shut off the alarm. I need a battery backup to prevent that, but with the holiday weekend, nothing is open to get one. Radio Shack advertised a big Memorial Day sale, but none of the stores I called answered the phone. I went to one twice, but they weren't open. And I am feeling depressed, smoldering with anger.

I am wondering what the difference is between yesterday and today in terms of my reaction. Yesterday, she wasn't nice to me, for one thing. She bitched me out for steaming the broccoli wrong, and spent the whole day reading a book while I did chores. We made love endlessly last night, but she went out anyway. Apparently, there's no relationship between those two things, but it pisses me off anyway.

I don't have much to do today. I did the laundry, and have been looking at women with the fantasy of picking one up. I'm only inches away from doing it, should the opportunity present itself. One time I told Rebecca that I hated it when her others "did it in my face," referring to nighttime escapades. She told me that since it wasn't happening in the apartment that it wasn't in my face. I don't know why I drew a distinction there, or why she picked up on it, but I'm sure that if I had outside sex "not in her face" that she would be very upset about it.

She said it as if it were excusable because it was outside of the apartment. It is so damned difficult for me to deal with. It's easier if it happens away from me, not on my time, so to speak, and especially easier if I don't know about it. Yet, yesterday I knew about it and it didn't bother me. Perhaps yesterday I didn't really believe that anything had happened the previous night. But she knows I'm getting the battery and that she will be trapped in the bedroom at night after that, and these are her last nights of freedom. She'll be out again tonight. The last night of freedom, because I'll get a battery tomorrow.

I woke up at 2:20 last night when she peed in the bucket. But I had been asleep soundly since about ten, and she could easily have come and gone in four hours.

Why did she look guilty this morning if she knows nothing about it? That really bugs me. She knows about it, more than she admits to me. Meanwhile, I look at everyone I see in the neighborhood with suspicion. I don't know who they are, and it could be all of them for all I know. She could be running little marathons every night. And I feel that everyone who looks at me is laughing at me for a fool. I'm the fool who's married to that woman who loves to fuck and suck, anyone and everyone. I'm angry and depressed today, both together. It's a shitty way to be. I don't like it.

I don't know the rules of this game, if there even are any. What am I supposed to find acceptable? What am

I supposed to tolerate? How much am I supposed to overlook and forgive? Who am I supposed to look in the eye without suspecting that they have sex with my wife? Why am I not supposed to have affairs, under these circumstances?

I feel like going down on as many women as I can find today. Just keep doing it. Even if they aren't particularly good-looking women. Have a marathon of my own. Do it until I cry. I want to cry. I picked up a hitchhiker once who offered me a blow job, and I turned him down. That's all he wanted, to do it to someone. I want to do it. At the rate Rebecca is going, it's only a matter of time before I get herpes and AIDS, so what the hell. She forgot to take her birth control pill this morning.

I'm sitting on the back porch, writing and smoking and drinking beer and listening to the two Chicanos who live in the basement wash their cars and play music on their box. If they are not involved with Rebecca, I don't know who is. The fat white one says hello to me when he walks by, and looks at me. I say hi back, but I don't smile. Mary says they deal dope, but I don't want to do business with them.

I haven't had any smoke for almost a month now, and I miss it right now. I've been wanting to learn to deal with this situation with a straight head, but right now I want to be high. I'm getting drunk instead. Fucking AC sent us an eviction notice a few weeks ago for non-payment of rent. He probably tore up the rent check just to piss me off. He for sure would know how to turn off the power in the basement, and Rebecca suggested that.

With a battery, I can keep her in at night; that will finally be foolproof. Without keys, there shouldn't be much else she can do in the apartment, unless of course AC or others have had keys made as fast as I can change the locks. I suppose I should go back to placing tape recorders just to reassure myself on that point, but they are so very difficult to listen to when there is shit evidence on them.

God, how I hate this whole situation. It is truly amazing to me that I love Rebecca enough to put up with this shit. Especially when, for all I know, she is shucking me, making a fool of me. Yes, there are many times when I suspect that she is conscious of more of her behavior than she lets on to me. It would be foolproof for her, as long as I can manage to at least suspect that she is innocent herself, that it is other personalities who are doing all this shit.

Meanwhile, I don't have a computer, and money keeps slipping away. My businesses are growing at the slowest possible pace. I will have to devote myself to doing a good job at DPH for at least a few more years in order to develop businesses I can live off of. It all sucks.

Vacation is over now, and I wonder if she was out every night and some of the days also. I wonder if it was really possible to restrain her other behavior during that time. I expected to see some pressure building up from restraint, but I'm not convinced there really was any restraint that amounted to anything. She probably got out every night.

Is it really possible for me to spend 24 hours a day with her to restrain her? And what would that accomplish? Would she just become bitchy and impossible to live with? Does she really have basic needs to let the others out? How long will it be before it is all under control? Will it ever be really under control? Will I spend the rest of my life living with a woman who is possessed by others, who can't survive without fucking around at every opportunity? What about me? Am I the sucker who plays along with this, providing the stability that permits this? What's in it for me? Good sex? Is that enough? And is it really that good when I am filled with resentment over her other behavior?

I told Dr. L that my life felt real now, as opposed to the artificial life I had been leading in my previous marriage. Is it real only because it hurts so much? Yes, Rebecca is fascinating, but can I take it? Yes, I can write about it, but isn't there a route to writing that doesn't involve so much suffering?

This life keeps me alone in the world. There is no one I can trust because he or she might be fucking my wife, or soon will be. Maybe that's not such a bad thing? That everybody fucks my wife? Maybe I can get used to that? After all, I fuck her as much as I want, and if there's a lot left over, is that so bad? God, I wish I knew what the rules were. This is fucked up.

Do I just say to myself, well, I have a wife who can't get enough, and I get as much as I can handle and so what if there's a lot of her left over for other people? It's such a beautiful day, and I feel so badly fucked up and miserable. I'm listening to the Chicanos vacuum out their cars, and it is a sound that I've heard on the tapes. Those damned tapes. Everybody is fucking Rebecca. She is sucking off every cunt and cock within her reach.

Damn, I wish I really knew the dimensions of it. I wish I knew who. For sure. I don't know what good that would do me, but at least I would be in on it. I hate being an outsider in this, I hate it passionately. Maybe I could laugh about it if I knew who. I don't know.

I'm going to meet her at work today, and I'm going to

be drunk. I'm going to say that I'm all screwed up today because she was out last night, that today I am angry and depressed about it instead of merely cerebral. I don't know what does any good. I don't know if my visible suffering has any dampening effect. I don't know if my complacency has any encouraging effect. I want to root out and kill those others who are making my life miserable. But I am completely helpless in the matter. There's nothing I can do except choose between suffering and being accepting of it.

There's a perfectly good lawn chair in the trash that I'm looking at, and there's also someone coming out of Heartland Drug with a new lawn chair. Does it make any sense? What makes sense? Does anything make sense? Did I really do the laundry this morning? Does clean underwear really matter that much? Did that woman with no wedding band want to fuck me? Does that black woman who's always sleepy want to fuck me? Should I? Why not? Would it help me? Her? Would it provide some sense of relief? It seems it would.

In 50 minutes, I leave to meet Rebecca at work. My free day will have ended. I will not have found any pussy. I will be up tight. I will want to fuck Rebecca just to get my share of her pussy. I want my share because I'm her husband. I want more than anyone else gets of her. Is that perverse? Is that a rotten reason for wanting to make love with her? Is she a community commodity? Am I a pushover for her? It's not easy. It's not easy. Dealing with Rebecca is not easy. She's supposed to be my wife. Mine. Exclusively. It's not easy knowing that there are streams of people sucking and fucking her. Her body. How am I supposed to differentiate between Rebecca and her body? Her others?

Now I have hiccups. The tree in front of me suddenly

has leaves, which blow in the breeze. They both have VW Rabbits, the Chicanos. One turns on his stereo and asks me if I like the music. It's okay. It's hard to type with hiccups. Let's see, six beers make me puke, and I've had three. I can have two more. I'm already drunk. And it's time to get number four.

The hiccups won't quit. They are getting out of control, like Rebecca's. She has hiccups and belches that rage out of control. I thought for a while that her hiccups coincided with shifts in personality, but I have forgotten to continue observing in that regard, so I don't know if it's true.

I wouldn't mind her having multiple personalities so much if only the others didn't want to do so much fucking and sucking. It's a violation of our relationship, at least of what I expect from our relationship. I want her total fidelity, and I can't have it, and I can't say anything about not having it. Yet she can bitch all she wants about the idea of me having outside relationships. I don't really want outside relationships, but part of me feels that fair is fair. If I have to allow her, why can't she allow me?

A couple is walking by. They probably don't have to give a thought to each other's faithfulness. Rebecca and I walk arm in arm down the street, but I am tortured by every glance we receive, suspecting that I'm seeing another secret sex partner of hers. Okay, so she is miserable about it.

Half an hour to go before I leave to meet her at work. Half an hour, and I will have her to myself for several hours. Until I fall asleep. Then she will be off again. Someone will turn off the power to the apartment and she will go off to someone, I don't know who, I don't know how many. I don't really know why. I just know that it tortures me. Some old Vietnamese guy is going through the garbage next door. My life seems like garbage. I'm going through one bag of garbage after another, day after day.

I am worrying about myself. There was a news article three weeks ago in the Globe, saying that abused children have difficulty forming a sense of identity. I can understand that. I wanted to discuss it in therapy, but two sessions went by and I never thought to bring it up. At the second session, I was agitated and anxious, talking widely and jumping quickly to other subjects.

Difficulty forming an identity. I talked about this with Rebecca last night, and she reinterpreted what I said, and said I had been a role player all my life, without ever developing my central self. I'm thinking about it a lot. I'm not really scared yet, but there is terror lurking. I have forgotten much of my life; I can remember much, but seldom do so spontaneously. It seems that each time I have decided to do a major role change, I have cast off the previous role and its contents, disowning it, forgetting it, being embarrassed by occasional memories of it.

I slip from one role into the next. What I said I accomplished in El Paso, that was stripping myself of roles completely, to find out who was left. Barely anyone was left. Barely anyone moved back to Boston, seeking to reclaim a lost beatnik life, seeking to return to that favored role, the starving but promising writer.

Displaying the same exotic expertise, card reading and metaphysical discussions in the 1960s, manuscript and metaphysical discussions in the 80s.

The favored role of someone whose whims are somehow godlike, and if not exactly godlike, tolerable with good humor. Adulation. People used to bring other people to meet me when I was a writer in the 60s. One time I was sitting nude at my desk working on some poems when a group of such people arrived. My nudity only added to my charisma. It's a damned likable role!

Playing a role is a curious thing for me because while I know it is acting, my acting is so complete that it takes me in. I am not only acting now, I am immersed into my role. Lost in it. I have no center from which to maintain simultaneous awareness of the various roles. And while that sounds scary to me, it doesn't really have me scared yet because I'm not really plugged into what this means. But underneath I think I must know, because underneath there is a creeping terror that has seized my neck muscles and they have ached badly for days. It's trying to leak through, trying to warn me that it's coming. I haven't seen enough of it yet to respond to it, but I'm slowly getting the message that this is a real warning of something awful.

In Texas, I finally realized that I could be anywhere and do anything I wanted. I chose to return to Boston and to pick up where I had left off as a creative writer. I chose the role I had left behind, the role whose freedom was offensive to my wife; for twenty years the role had been shut off.

Parts of it continued but were diverted into available opportunities, particularly writing. The final discovery that I was a successful financial consultant sent my head spinning. The role seemed so real. I knew deep inside of myself that this success meant I could get divorced; knew it long before it reached my mind in words.

I had taken on the role of father, cutting much too short that blissful period we enjoyed before the birth. That was a difficult period, financially. I decided to take on a role that would brand me with a job—printer. But I got little work to do. Still, I immersed myself deeper into my printer role, as if to magnify it and make it attract business.

Being a successful financial consultant, though, that was really spectacular for me! I had never felt as truly successful before. It was status, income, a generous role! And I didn't let go of it easily! Circumstances did that. But at least I know that I am able to play such a role.

When I was doing a lot of acting in college, I had an enlightening realization one night on stage, when I found myself so completely into my character that I wasn't sure who I really was; that who I thought I really was was just another role I played. I assumed anyone would come to that realization after doing a certain amount of acting.

Sometimes I am the life of the party. Sometimes I am the wallflower, bored and want to go home. The party can be the same. It's not all the same me because I can't reach one from the other. It just all depends on which me arrives at the party.

When it's the party me, I am peaked out on funny things to say and alert to every opportunity to be entertaining. The alternate is usually very formal and reserved. Isn't that astonishing to realize?

Leslie used to marvel at how I chose "crazy" girls to mess around with. She didn't understand what attracted me to them nor how I could stand them. But if I group myself among them, then it becomes understandable. Crazies can understand other crazies.

I have been wondering if our enormous attraction to each other, Rebecca and I, was based on our similar personality problems, that somehow our total beings saw themselves in each other, at least more clearly than they had ever before, and quickly joined forces.

The superficial evidence would not tend to support this idea; I am supposing that there is something big operating below our level of awareness, beneath the superficial, something that can look through our eyes and form weightier opinions than our conscious ones, something we call the unconscious to which we attribute much, something big, something whose influence upon our minds and behaviors is a concept we are only beginning to grasp. Is that me?

I have had a number of perceptions this evening, while high, and I am trying to remember them. One was while talking with Rebecca after supper. She described, as she often has, feeling overwhelmed by everything, including the least little thing. I commented that it sounded like she was a little girl, looking into an adult world. I suggested that she doesn't have to assume she is responsible for any tasks because those are handled by adults; she can relax.

Rebecca wove into the conversation mention of the fact that there was a breath left for a message yesterday on the answering machine, and a no-message today, while we have gone for weeks without any unexpected messages. Also wove in mention of Mitch. It occurred to me that THIS is the

Rebecca who has sexual encounters, or at least it's one of them, but this one would be so simple to take advantage of. Unable to cope, unable to resist. She must be very young, perhaps four.

But I was really referring to perceptions about myself, none of which have yet occurred to me, but which I have experienced today. I am thinking right now that with Rebecca, multiple personalities and repressed memories may be two different problems. If that were true, I could believe that I am equally as multiple personalitied as she is. I have been realizing today how very different I've been upon arriving at work on various mornings. It has ranged from hilarious happiness to depression, with angry and bewildered and others thrown in.

Of course, I am thinking about that very difficult two-month period during which we were making the tape recordings and dealing with the evidence, and I was going through a wide variety of reactions. But even so, looking back at my life, I have exhibited quite a range of behaviors, each of them assuming it was me.

When I was the guru's group leader, there were times when I followed the teachings, and many times that were kept distinctly separate when I didn't, like having affairs with six of the women in the group. A day arrived. I had been faithfully not thinking of getting involved with any of those women. A day arrived when, seemingly without thinking a single thought, I opened my arms to Pam, she looked at me, asked incredulously, "Me?" and came to me.

I had begun to use the power I had developed over them. Next was Norma. Then Sam. Then Jane. Then Ileane. Then Jan. All without thought, all a complete turnabout from where I had been a second before. By

86

the time I got to Jan, the second virgin, I had lost patience and was not gentle and supportive; rather, I was harsh and demanding. And it was not successful sex. I spoiled a wonderful thing with Pam, too, by being demanding and insensitive.

I've never truly recognized another's feelings until Rebecca came along. And I'm afraid of all of my own feelings that are stored up somewhere, waiting to register on me. I need to win the megabucks so I can afford to let that happen.

I was accused non-stop of being forgetful at home in Urbana, and I was, extremely so. Very often, there were things from the previous week, even the previous day, that I could not recall. Leslie and Hector were always amazed. Hector called me dumb, just like my art teacher used to call be dumb for being colorblind. I never stopped to wonder about it, never let it bother me. The lost memories were usually of daily family conversation, and I considered them no great loss, although it is curious to me now that I didn't wonder more then about having such a faulty memory.

I didn't get angry with Rebecca during our first month together. And I was genuinely comfortable with that. But then I got angry the first time, then again, and there were real depths to my anger. Is this the same person?

I read an article on loneliness in *Psychology Today*. It was about me. Talked about reluctance in approaching strangers, doubts about forming an intimate relationship. And it was about Rebecca, too. She and I are stopgaps for each other, everything we need to fight off the loneliness, for as long as we can make it last, or perhaps until we learn an antidote to loneliness.

She and I match each other in so many ways. That is why we fit together, because we each need to be matched in many ways, and we are able to match in those ways. Tonight, she was a romantic housewife, very loving and sweet, demure. Last night she was a little child, frightened, overwhelmed.

I was in a stupor at breakfast this morning when a subtle shift clicked into place in my head, and I was suddenly more alert and aware of my responsibilities to myself. It helped me into the day. I did a good day's work in half a day, got restless and came home early.

We are taking off work today (Sunday) because Rebecca couldn't handle going in. We've been slowly mellowing out together somewhat. It's nearly impossible to maintain a feeling of closeness between us; we can experience it, but we can't seem to sustain it. And so things get to what seems to be critical proportions, and sheer need drives us together again, and we open up with each other.

I have stayed high today, but have smoke that seems high in CBD, giving me a spacey feeling in addition to a sharpened concentration and enhanced insight and memory. I have caught glimpses of the person I could be, and it makes me gulp and want to cry. I could be caring, outgoing, friendly, interesting, dashing. I could be at ease on stage or in public. I could be respected and admired. I could be superior to most other people, if only I could let go of my conviction that I can never really accomplish any serious superiority of any sort.

I am realizing that I have been stopped up in expressing my love to Rebecca, that the wonderful, free-flowing, profuse loving I gave her earlier is still in me, wanting to come out, but that it is being held in check because now there are things to fear. We were carefree, relatively speaking, in those earlier days of our love. Everything was looking up. It was a good time. These days are filled with specters, fears and terrors that lurk, waiting.

There were times I feared for my life with Rebecca. I went to bed nights fully convinced that she would knife me to death before morning. But I loved her so completely that I couldn't do otherwise than go to bed with her.

At other times, I feared for my life through tortuous emotional abuse at her hand. I just flat-out knew that she was going to kill me. I faced that fear, I remember, by saying: so what? Can I do that now? Can I really say "so what?" to all of my fears?

I've been home from work sick yesterday and today. It is a bizarre kind of sick. Saturday night, I pulled down the window shade, then felt a draft brush my right side. My first impression was that it was a draft from the window, but it kept on entering my body, and it felt like a ghost had walked into me.

I began shivering uncontrollably, feeling very chilled. But that was all; the rest of me wasn't affected. I just looked at this curious thing happening to my body. I went to bed and shivered a lot. The uncontrollable part only lasted about two minutes. And I sweated vast quantities.

Yesterday, we checked my temperature and I had a two-degree fever. It's down a little today, and I sweated profusely last night again, so much that Rebecca made me change clothes and she spread my terry cloth bathrobe out under me in the middle of the night. So my head is a little woozy from a slight fever, and I decided I would try to write anyway.

So it seems that I have permitted Rebecca to choose to keep her illness. It hadn't occurred to me at all that such a choice was even possible for me, that it would even be considered. I didn't even think I was facing a "choice" situation. It seemed to me that there was a road that went onward and upward, and that was that.

Who would not choose such a road? Rebecca, for one. She has chosen against the road onward and upward, the road which might have held genuine hope for a resolution of her personality problems, and she has chosen instead to keep her problems. She thinks it is for a while longer, but I certainly know better, and suspect that deep inside of her, she knows too.

Mrs. Hyde prevailed and won the decision that saved her life, won her reprieve, won survival for herself and the others. And I have permitted this choice. Not gracefully at all; I have made it high-handedly clear to her that I am not in support of her choice, and have been very angry with her about it. Yet in the end, I believe that I permitted it. I had to. It is ultimately her life, not mine. And how can I insist that she take on a burden that I cannot really help her with?

But in permitting it, I have deprived myself of a great deal. The champion Rebecca, undauntable, is gone. The woman with a strong career future is gone. The company I will have will always be about what it is now—a quiet shadow in the house; now a hungry, needy, poor pitiful wet kitten; a wound-up robot playing a record of the day; a lost, faraway shell doing dishes; a timid voice too soft to hear with nothing to say, but wanting to touch me; an oddly hung-up sexual partner who holds tightly certain reins within herself with unpredictable results. The parts that commanded my great respect are gone. Now I have a companion who needs care like a pet.

I told my therapist that I was on the verge of deciding, and perhaps had in fact already decided, that I could no longer endure my relationship with Rebecca. I explained the whole thing about her reaction to the specialist's insistence that she undergo a series of termination appointments with her previous therapist before she began seeing him. About how I had done everything I could to steer her away from her lousy decision except to cram it down her throat.

I said I was only about 85% sure that I was right, and that as long as I felt even some doubt, I had to allow her the right to make her own decision because it is her life that is at risk. My therapist commented that it was interesting that I was willing to terminate the relationship, but was not willing to cram down her throat my strong feeling that she should do the series of termination appointments.

He pointed out that if the cramming didn't work, the relationship would be terminated anyway, ending up at the same place with nothing more lost. So I thought about that and decided to give her the ultimatum that she choose to follow the specialist's advice before the end of the month, or on August 1st I would contact an attorney about a divorce, and that August 31st would be moving day, with her finding her own arrangements. I did this Wednesday; today is Friday.

Day by day, she is looking for me to weaken in my resolve. My anger has abated, but my resolve has not. It is very frightening for me, because I love her so much and am terrified at the prospect of losing her. I have to keep reminding myself that I have already lost her if she doesn't give in to me and the specialist.

We haven't been sleeping together, or even touching, since about last Saturday. In the afternoon, she invited me to bed with her, then steered the discussion to how she felt I was using her. I had to think about that, about whether or not to answer her honestly. Because, of course, part of me does feel that I am using her. And that she is using me. Not in any harmful sense, but in the strictly literal sense, yes. So she decided she wouldn't make love with me.

That night, I attempted to approach her and she continued to refuse. So in my stubborn, hurt way, I have since refused to touch her. I have already lost all of that wonderful love-making, love-making that I have never experienced before and may never again.

One of her interpretations of my insistence that she follow the specialist's advice was that I just wanted to control her, that I was angry because she wasn't in my control. I told her that I wanted her to survive her life. It's curious, though, how very much she tries to control me, and in fact how much I have allowed her to control me. She sees nothing wrong in that. But she won't allow herself to be controlled.

This morning, Rebecca proposed to me that we have a temporary arrangement where she would move into the new apartment with me as a roommate, sharing expenses, to give her time to make arrangements for going out on her own. I am thinking about it, and was thinking about it before she mentioned it, for that matter. It will be a terrible loss to me when she leaves, and the prospect of having her stay with me a while longer has its appeal. But I can't stand living with her any more. I am thinking that we need to renegotiate an entirely new basis for a relationship, and I am trying to figure out what the features would be.

It seems definite to me that a divorce is a must, even if that's all that changes. I cannot bear the humiliation of being husband to this woman. I have been faithful to her since I met her, while she has been having sex with men, women and children at virtually every opportunity, and probably several times a day. I can't stand the thought that all of those people know me, or about me, and I don't know them, that they mess with my things, steal, burglarize, some of my things, generally invade my privacy, particularly the privacy of my wife's body.

I've never slept with a whore, so I don't know anything about the feeling of having a woman who just left another man an hour or so ago. But I do know the torture of touching Rebecca's pubic hair and feeling it matted up from stickiness. And the gnawing, burning suspicions that plague me whenever she takes a shower at an unusual time, like the other noon when I came home for lunch and she had been home sick. The very first thing she did when I got home was go into the shower. It was as if I hadn't come home to see her at all, but that I was just stopping by to check the mail or something.

I know the agony of having her call me at work with some trivial, trumped up excuse for calling, which we had determined some months before to be her signal that something was going on and she needed to know that I couldn't be home any sooner than half an hour from downtown so I wouldn't walk in and catch her. It's amazing to me, come to think of it, that I have never caught her. Seems to be against probabilities.

So divorce would give me a sense of distance from her so that these kinds of things wouldn't be a constant torture to me. I think. There remains the fact that I love her very much. And it isn't fair that she have all of this sex with other people, regardless of her excuse, good as it is, with me being faithful to her.

I need the same freedom, the freedom that I am forced to give her against all of my will. Somehow, against all of her will, I must win the same freedom from her. I don't know how much I would actually use such freedom, but knowing I have it would relieve a great deal of the pressure. Plus, if I did have other sexual relationships, I think it would again give me a little additional distance from Rebecca.

So if she were my roommate, not my wife, and had no right to restrict my freedoms, and if she were also willing to have sex with me, if only on a recreational basis, perhaps we could have a relationship that I could tolerate. I wonder.

I wonder if I could handle having her live with me without us having sex. It would kill me if she ever brought someone to her room, although I would welcome the opportunity to bring someone to my room.

Is it such a bad thing for a woman to give in to her man? Rebecca knows nothing of compromise. She must control our relationship, overtly or covertly as in pussy-whipping. When it comes to irreconcilable differences, is it so terrible for a wife to give in to her husband? Must the relationship end instead? Women have given in to husbands for generations; why is it suddenly such a terrible thing?

I've been thinking of asking Rebecca for a fair hearing. So far, her reactions to the specialist and to me have been highly emotional. She has not listened to either of us reasonably. I'd like to ask her to listen to me without instantly rejecting what I have to say, without instantly striking out at what I say. I'd like her to consider that I am an intelligent and mature person, that I am not handicapped by any mental illness, that I am a competent person, that I am a good analyst, that I love her and wish her the best things.

I'd like her to consider that I am very possibly correct in what I say, that I am worth giving in to. I'd like her to consider that it is possible for her to be wrong, especially when she is being led by her emotions which are her problem area, not her strength.

I'm all over the wall with my thoughts. I don't know how to handle this situation. Getting out of it altogether seems to be a very ready solution, but it is so expensive—Rebecca is, I'm sure, irreplaceable. I'll spend the rest of my life remembering her, comparing every future woman against her and being disappointed. I can become wealthy and alluring to women, and I can have all the sex I want; but will I ever find such love again, and will I ever find such wonderful sex again?

But, I have already lost these, and am only wishing that I hadn't. They are already gone, and the best I can do now is to salvage what I can of the situation, or else chuck the whole thing. I can't hope ever to regain what we have lost, unless she gives in to me and does what the specialist says.

When she proposed the temporary arrangement of living with me, she was of course suggesting that she use me for her own advantage. That's an important bargaining point, if I can get her to acknowledge it. What is the advantage to me? She'd contribute toward costs; money. In this very troubled situation, money is not really all that attractive to me as an incentive. It's sort of a minor point.

Maybe she thinks that if she can only buy enough time, she can somehow win me back. If so, that's another advantage to her. Where's my advantage? Sure, I'd love to have our relationship in full bloom again, but is there really any chance of that unless she gets back into the race and begins showing her championship colors again?

In any event, a temporary arrangement that didn't frustrate both of us to death would at least prolong hope that someday we could marry again, someday when she finally resolved her multiple personality problems.

All of the rules of the game got changed when we found out that Rebecca was an active multiple personality. Up to that time, I had been completely dedicated and devoted to her, submerged in my love for her, happy to have my life revolve only around her and little else. I was fully committed to her and to her welfare.

I had passed through a number of ways of coping with her outside sexual activity. At first, I thought I should pimp her; that was an angry reaction, as most of my reactions were. Then, I thought I should share her; I told her at the time that every man within reach should have a shot at her pussy because it was so wonderful.

Then I began a long series of thwarting techniques, attempting to restrain her outside sex, but it was finally fruitless; she found ways of outwitting me every time. Then, I sought the best specialist for her that I could find; she rejected him with all of her might. I tried to force her to change her mind, to make what I was certain was the right decision, to follow the specialist's clear-cut course of action, and she rejected this also, rejecting me in the process, accusing me of wanting to control her.

And now, I must let her live with her decision. She is very wrong, but I have exhausted my possibilities. I can see no hope for her. She cannot allow herself to rely on anyone else's judgment, not even mine. I feel that reduces me to one of her conveniences, and that only when she feels like it.

I am half-packed, ready to move at the end of the month. She is stumbling around, trying to hold the pieces of her life together, trying to get an apartment with two girlfriends. She has little time to do it, and has gotten off to a very slow start. She may not end up with a place to live, and I half expect that she will make an emergency appeal to me at the last minute to move into my new apartment with me.

In the meantime, I pace the apartment, waiting for the end of the month to arrive. This will go on for 27 days. Then I will know what she is going to do, and what my life will be like in the immediate future. We talk very little now, mostly chit-chat. She is having a lot of difficulty dealing with the ending of our relationship. I am fighting off depression, tears, fears of loneliness, regrets, guilt over abandoning her; lots of feelings.

The rules changed. Suddenly, I was no longer able to permit her full freedom to make her own decisions. Suddenly, it was not mere guidance that my role consisted of. I had to steer her course by force, as much force as I could bring to bear, because I knew it would take at least all of that to budge her; and it wasn't enough. She is firmly locked into her mistrust of me, of anyone. I wasn't able to break that.

Perhaps, with the new rules in the forefront now, she will be able to find a man who can tolerate her problem behavior, one who will be in the position of knowing what he is getting into. I didn't. Of course, she didn't either. As I say, the rules changed, for both of us.

She thought she was being faithful to me, and I thought so, too. She still has great difficulty seeing that she has not been, cannot see that it is a part of herself. She sees it almost as if it is someone else's problem, not hers, and therefore thinks it shouldn't be my problem, either. But it is, of course. She does not claim any ownership of her other personalities, but if they are not hers, whose are they? They're not mine or anyone else's.

I saw a lawyer Friday after work, and he felt that there were probably enough grounds to get an annulment, but he wanted a thousand dollars to handle it, and I can't afford that. I will look for a cheaper lawyer next week.

Last night, Rebecca slept over at her friend Judy's. They stopped by the apartment briefly during the evening while I was sitting on the steps with some neighbors. As they were leaving, Judy said, "We're going to eat," and she stuck out her tongue and wiggled it. Sarcastically, I said, "I know!" Rebecca says I'm not supposed to interpret this as a sexual relationship.

I am very hurt by it. I can't wait for August to go by so I won't know what Rebecca is up to, anymore than she is aware.

God, I feel awful. Life sucks and you die.

Last night, Rebecca's climax when I went down on her looked and sounded like her fifth or sixth rather than her first. She said Mary was in the apartment Friday, Rebecca's day off. About two joints worth of my pot was missing, taken sometime between bedtime Friday and Saturday afternoon. Rebecca, who never smokes pot, has a roach burn on her lip which she is calling chapping or something.

She said Mary was on the phone Friday, but the call was not taped, though the calls before and after were. So the machine was paused if Mary called, which Rebecca doesn't even think to do for herself. She was drooping and shuffling when I got home Friday, which seems to be a sign that something has occurred and been repressed. Lately, she has been asking me how I slept. I think an other was messing around with Mary during the day Friday, and again during the night. Friday night, Rebecca provided the pot.

It just keeps happening.

When I told her the pot was missing, she accused Mary of it, saying she had left Mary alone at the phone on my desk while she had gone into the kitchen. I wonder how much of a scapegoat she might be making of Mary?

Yesterday, the phone rang and hung up when I, a man, answered it. Rebecca says I read too much into things. Well, I'm flexible on that one.

We discussed the possibility of having a third person live with us. Rebecca had been telling me about her impression that Amy was feeling very relieved to see that Rebecca deals with Trisha, that she had been reluctant to share her apartment only with Trisha earlier, and that it was she, Rebecca, who as a third person was making the important difference in the situation. So, I suggested that perhaps what we needed was a third person, giving rise to an idea we had both given lots of thought to but which we hadn't admitted yet to each other. The idea was that Rebecca and Trisha could both move into my new apartment with me. It had its appeal to me, and I had several restrictions in mind that would have to be acceptable before I would consider it. Rebecca raised the idea. She had not identified the problems, and presented the idea to me as a wholesome solution.

I parried by pretending to be thinking deeply about it, considering it as a new idea. I ended up saying that it would depend on establishing adequate distance for me, which meant that she would sleep in her bedroom shared with Trisha, that my office and bedroom would be off-limits for security reasons. She had in mind that she would be sharing my bed under this arrangement.

I told her I saw the problems as being that I would seduce Trisha sooner or later, and perhaps fall in love with her; and that, regardless of how well the situation was arranged, I wouldn't have the distance I must have.

We agreed to live apart and that she would spend her weekends off with me.

We have been much friendlier since, although she is going through a lot of turmoil dealing with the upcoming change.

Rebecca described, guided by my questioning, three types of memory she has. The first is ordinary, actual memory. The second is fragmentary memory, actually remembered bits and pieces but with important parts missing, particularly actual traumas, and this is seen as a less trustworthy type of memory. The third kind is non-specific in terms of actual memories, but rather is a body of knowing, where memories that are hidden from specificity are translated into bodies of knowledge. She distributes her memories as 50% actual, 25% fragmentary, and 25% knowledge.

Half of her life has been spent in other personalities where memories arc kept separately, it would appear.

We went shopping this morning for some shoes for Rebecca, at the New Balance factory outlet. When we entered, she said later, she felt like a lost little girl, and wouldn't be left alone to shop, but came to my side instead. I asked later if it seemed she was experiencing other personalities consciously at a greater rate. She felt this was true.

She asked at breakfast what I thought of my therapist pointing out that Rebecca didn't have anyone in her taking responsibility for the actions of the others, or feeling any guilt. He said this illustrated the fact that she is not an integrated personality. I told her that it made me take her less seriously. I can expand now that I meant on a moment-to-moment basis, that I would relate to her as I saw her over time, more so than on the basis of the present moment. I wouldn't take her deep suicidal depressions quite as seriously, but would see that they pass and seem to leave no mark on her. I needn't be saving her life; it saves itself.

It will be only a few more weeks before I have my new computer, and I am anxious to begin organizing my notes about Rebecca and begin work on a novel. I have quite a stack of printout and diskettes to wade through.

Rebecca told me today that she is often afraid of sex, and doesn't approach me at such times because she doesn't want to get anything started. I told her it was a little girl who needed to learn that there can be good sex as well as bad.

There were two people at my burglary. Since when do burglars work in teams? God, I miss that Kaypro II. It was such a sweet little computer. The green phosphor screen was so very pleasant to watch as images faded in and out. The characters were small, and accumulated peacefully on the screen. And the keyboard had such a wonderful sound, so clunky and mechanical. It told me very clearly that I was the man and that it was the machine.

My insight into and understanding of Rebecca seem to be developing rapidly. In the back of my mind, there is this idea that if I could understand her well enough to deal with her without getting hurt, I could have her live with me. I'm going to miss her so much. Most of the time lately, I have been watching women with the thought of starting up some affairs. The rest of the time, I see myself bending more dearly to my purpose, taking what comes my way without becoming distracted. I can use diversion, but not distraction. But I really feel ambivalent about starting up with other women. My impulses all stop short.

I am in a quiet, relatively peaceful, good mood today. I am feeling much less troubled.

There are times when Rebecca needs to be seduced, I am now realizing, because she is a shy young girl. I could get into that. It occurs to me how much it would help to be able to identify ahead of time who I am going to be sleeping with tonight, rather than try to enforce my expectations. Maybe Dr. L was wrong when he told me to just treat her as my wife, making no special recognition of her variations. Maybe trying to follow that advice is what's gotten me into so much trouble with this relationship.

Right now, Rebecca is meeting Trisha to go to Amy's and settle details of moving in there. I just know that she will come back with a story that says it can't work out. I just know that she will wangle her way into my new apartment; it's her last hope. And part of me will be glad. Maybe I can learn to manage the relationship, rather than letting her control it, I tell myself. It would be a god-awful amount of work; would it be worth it? In many ways, yes.

I am quite high right now. I smoked up this morning, then was sitting on the front steps and Michael called out his window for me to come up, and handed me two nice buds which I cleaned and rolled into two bones. It was good, somewhat slow to take effect, and has shot me up much higher. I sat on his floor for a while, and a stream of others gradually appeared, filling the apartment. After about two hours, I left and came downstairs, where I am now, writing this. I am slightly shaky, and am a little jumpy and nervous. I am zipping around in my head.

I came into the apartment thinking that Rebecca probably wouldn't be home from her thing with Trisha and Amy for another hour or two at least, and ended up in the kitchen wondering why she was late coming home from work! Even as I write this, it is interrupted by side-tracks. The neighbor's stereo is loud, playing Dear Eddie from the sixties, and I know the tune, and I begin swaying to it, letting my imagination float along with it, until the blinking cursor finally penetrates my vision and reminds me that I am writing. Eddie my love, the song says. Please, Eddie, don't make me wait too long. I'm still trying to discern the rationale behind the vegetarian diet I stuck to for 19 years. Zapping around like that.

Upstairs, a stream of others came in and made up the company. It had been just Michael and myself, plus what's-her-name in the background, and then I felt displaced, cautious among strangers. I felt they had taken Michael away from me. It's a parallel to relating to Rebecca.

I went out to buy pipe cleaners today, and I failed. Two stores didn't have them, and I sailed past the third without going in and was most of the way home before I realized it. I had bought a box of peppermint patties and a cigarette lighter on my rounds.

I needed to learn that a person can indeed learn to deal with a mate who has extramarital sex, so that I could stop feeling guilty about having hurt Leslie. It is possible, was possible, for her to learn how to deal with me. And apparently she found the way.

If I give up some of my values, I can deal with Rebecca. And, I now realize, this is what has been rummaging around in the back of my mind these last few weeks. Part of me is saying that giving up values is a reasonable thing to do. And part of me is resistant as hell. And just now it is easy for me to see that it is the dying part of me resisting, and the growing part of me changing; that there is really no reasonable choice other than to consider the surrender of certain values as reasonable. And that seems so topsy-turvy to me that it spins in my mind. And I wonder if Rebecca is going through something similar.

What values would I have to give up? First, that I have a natural right to exclusive access to my wife's body. When Dr. L said to me, "You have a right to expect monogamy in your marriage," I didn't understand it as a challenge. I used it as a crutch instead. Where is my right, when I myself took that right away from Leslie? No, I don't have a right to a monogamous marriage. That is a value that would have to go.

Then, there is my right to expect Rebecca to be what I want her to be. Instead, I would have to permit her to be who she is, even though there are things about her that I find very offensive and feel compelled to correct. Instead, I would have to be very tolerant of her, granting her my full permission to be herself, without regard for how that might reflect upon me or my feelings or my reputation. That is a very big bite to take.

God, this place is suddenly empty. It is 7:30 in the evening; Rebecca moved out about 6:45. I went to the new apartment to find out about keys and scheduling my move, called my man and van, bought some beer, and just now walked in.

Rebecca made one last try to cancel the separation. She told me repeatedly that she saw it as just a cop-out on my part. It was a lousy attempt, but I almost gave in anyway, just because I am going to miss her so intensely.

Amy was almost two hours late getting here with the van, and I brought in two dinners from Deli King. It only took moments to load her stuff into the van, including two dressers; and then she was gone. We kissed goodbye, but not passionately. I promised to call her Tuesday evening. We will see each other next weekend. I waved goodbye to her three times. When she hopped into the passenger seat of the van, she broke into a big smile, but then she let it fade away. I think we both have genuinely mixed feelings about this separation. I certainly do, and she certainly must. Now, I have to begin packing and taking things apart for the move, for tomorrow is my day. I just saw the apartment, and it shrank since I saw it last.

I am having blind spots in my memory. I fixed my desk file drawer so it wouldn't lock, because there is no way to unlock it. I had to puzzle over it for some time before I figured out an easy way to do it. Later, I opened the file drawer and remembered that I had fixed it, but could not remember how. It was much later, after wondering about it a lot, that I remembered—I pulled out the spring clip that engages the locking arm.

If I am having blind spots, it is because I am denying memories. I have been depressed as well as in shock since the separation and move, and I think that during depression I tend to deny my memories because they are imbued with depression.

I am denying memories, then, I assume. I searched and searched for the surveillance tapes and just now found them. I figured out that they were in a box rather than a garbage bag, because I was in the kitchen and noticed that my knife block wasn't there, and I remembered distinctly that it had been packed in a box. But I had been through all of the boxes at least twice, making sure they were all unpacked and it seemed they were. But there was a Hammermill Paper box on the dresser, the bottom box of a stack, which was never unpacked. I can't remember why I didn't open it up until just now, why I deliberately overlooked it, in spite of my efforts to find it. And in that box were the tapes. I can't remember what was in my mind when I came to that box each time. It is very fuzzy, like, oh, I know what that is.

Rebecca was discharged from the hospital yesterday afternoon; I found out by calling there. Today, she left a message for me to call, and I did. She ended up hanging up on me again over discussion of me possibly having sexual affairs. I was being angry with her, basically taunting her. I want her to learn to deal with it somehow, whether I actually do it or not. But it is also a good excuse to get angry at her, telling her that if I have to accept it in her, then she has to accept it in me. I didn't say that, but that's what it boils down to.

The funny thing is, I think I can accept it in her. I don't yet, but it could be possible. And it would be great if she could also accept it in me.

I had a therapy appointment this morning. I talked about everything, jumping from subject to subject. I told Dr. L that I had thought about the statement he once made that I have a right to a monogamous marriage. I said that I had been questioning my right to such a relationship, because I had denied it to Leslie.

He identified this as an interesting statement and drew me out more on it. I came up with half a dozen ways of looking at it. He said that I was at the extreme end of a spectrum when it comes to tolerance, that most any other man would simply separate from a wife who was unfaithful. He also said that the vast majority of women would be faithful to their man.

Near the end of the session, I asked, "Rebecca's not going to change, is she?" He said, "It's going to be a long, hard, slow process for her." I said, "And she's not trying very hard." I broke out crying, realizing that she was gone, that I would never again have that intimate, loving relationship with her. She will be my occasional guest, and we will pretend, both of us, that we will be able to reconcile our relationship.

I phoned her late this afternoon to see how she was feeling, to see if she was up to visiting me this weekend. She plans to come over tomorrow night, stay two nights, and leave for work from here Monday morning. I'm looking forward to it, although with fresh stitches from a laparoscopy, she may not be in very good condition for love-making.

Rebecca arrived Saturday in time for supper, and we had a very pleasant weekend. For love-making, we stuck with oral sex because she is still healing from her surgery. She is coming again Thursday night. We'll see how it goes.

I am feeling much calmer, but my energy level is very low. I am physically exhausted and filled with arthritic pains. It was a very rough week, last week. Now, I am tired out, able to do my job but not with enthusiasm.

Rebecca isn't coming over tonight. We had arranged it last weekend that she would come here after work and spend the night, leaving in the morning for her therapy appointment. But when I got home, the answering machine had a message from her saying she wasn't feeling well.

It was an odd message in the way it was delivered. "Hi, George, this is Rebecca. I'm leaving a message on your machine for you that I'm not feeling very well, that I won't be able to make it out to see you this evening, um, if you give me a call, um this evening after six at 628, um, 5528, and we can arrange for another time. Thank you."

It was brisk and businesslike. It was one of the others. And I am fantasizing that she is going out after work with Mitch in preference to visiting me, and it makes me want to get angry. I tell myself that if there are obstacles to the reality I want, it is because I am maladroit at creating reality at this point, and that I still need, temporarily I hope, to juggle and outwit the obstacles in my way. But that urge to become angry wells up in heaves, wanting to get out. And I am holding it back. It makes me want to cry.

Can I give her up? I was really looking forward to her visit. I was thinking that, if I could have my life pretty much to myself, that it would be wonderful to have her back. But I tend to bury all of the bad things about her, and romanticize the wonderful things, and I end up with an image of how she would be ideally, for me. And of course it's not true.

She's not coming over tonight, for example. Unless that is only an obstacle, a flaw in one of the facets of my created reality. But can I give her up? Can I face never seeing her again, never making love with her again? The thought of seeing her on her next visit sustains me. It keeps me satisfied. But without that prospect, will I be haunted by loneliness? Will I become desperate and begin entertaining women beneath my usual taste? I'm afraid of that idea just now.

I made orange juice for her. And she didn't show up. She gave me all this shit over the phone, exaggerated ideas, testing me, cursing me for the way she interpreted the results, demanding that she have everything she feels entitled to from me—completeness to our relationship.

She didn't come over, and I was disappointed. I had done the dishes, and made sure the place was straightened up for her. I'd been thinking of her visit all day. I planned our dinner together.

And I made orange juice. All for her. I didn't eat the meal myself. She's actually crazy. Her feelings are rampantly out of control, and they whip her in all directions. And she calls me and demands that I be fully accepting of that, fully understanding and supportive of her. She is a crazy person. I have to face that; I can't avoid it any longer.

I have figured out how Rebecca manipulates me. It is one of those things that was right before my eyes all along, but I never looked squarely at it. Whenever I give in to what she wants, she is happy. Whenever I do not, she is unhappy. Because I have found delight and satisfaction in making her happy, I have routinely given in to her wishes all along.

But in the process, the question of what makes me happy has never come up, other than the pleasure I get from making her happy. She has never given in to me on anything significant, and in the few little things where she has given in, it has been with petulance or a blanking out of all feeling, unless it is something she simply has no feeling about. Grocery shopping is a good example. I choose generic or house brands while she prefers name brands. She feels slighted when I insist on a cheaper brand; other times, she goes into a blank mood.

I am attempting to make the resolve that when something is important to me and my choice makes her unhappy, I will just let her be unhappy. I wish to put a stop to her manipulations of me.

Two days ago, I came home early from work and cried my heart out for half an hour, the first real crying I have done since I was a child. That evening, we once again reviewed the situation, and I finally gave in on a major point—we could allow the relationship more time, but we would live apart. She seemed to be very happy with this; I had given in to her. But it was only one of the items on her agenda.

She brought up the subject of moving in with me. I explained my reasons for objecting to that, and she seemed to accept them. But last night, it came up again, this time with force. She had only postponed that agenda item for one night. She had not been sincere in our agreement of the night before. I refused to agree to let her live with me, and she got unhappy. I felt very sorry that she was unhappy, and felt guilty about making her unhappy. But today, I see that it is all manipulation, and I won't stand for it.

My reasons for objecting to having her live with me are that I can't stand to watch her life as it is being lived; I feel too betrayed, too helpless, and feel that her situation is too hopeless. I need distance from her so that I am not being forced to observe her live. I can deal with visits from her, with her accounts of events past; but I cannot watch events as they are unfolding.

It is like the difference between visiting the site of a battle and being in the battle itself. Also, I need space to develop my own life, something I do not have when we are living together because all of our attention is focused on her life. It is always her needs that we are dealing with, almost never my needs. I need room for outside friendships, something she has effectively prohibited me from having, even at long distance. Also, I need to stop dedicating myself to a losing cause. I must at least save myself.

We went for two weeks without making love. We barely talked. She went through an elaborate charade of organizing two other women to rent our apartment when I move out, a charade full of flaws which I pointed out as it progressed, but she completely discounted anything I had to say about it.

I wanted it to work for her; she didn't. She wanted it to fail so that she would be abandoned and helpless if I didn't take her in with me in the new apartment. And I know I can't refuse to take her in, at least temporarily. But I will make her life miserable, just to force her to find other accommodations.

She has been accusing me of being a knight in shining white armor, out to save her. She insists that she doesn't need my help. I admit to the charge, because, under the circumstances, she needs so much help and there is a great deal of help that I am able to give her, but which she is unable to accept from me.

She sees it as an attempt to get her under my control.

I see it as an attempt to encourage her growth into a together adult human being. She wants us to be equals, even in areas where we clearly are not. She does not trust me or my ability to think and see things clearly. She doesn't trust my maturity, my experience, my knowledge. It is all unrecognizable to her. That is, she stubbornly refuses to recognize it. She is plagued with pride of enormous proportions.

I have so many beautiful memories of Rebecca. I will certainly treasure them all. My drive wants to sever all memory of her, but I won't accept that this time. There are many bad memories, and I'll let go of those as well as I can. But I want to hold those wonderful, blissful moments in my memory for the future. They are precious.

Never before had I experienced such sheer joy and satisfaction. She can be very wonderful. But only in memory for me, for I have told her that I never want to see her again, in a letter I wrote tonight in reply to hers asking for a divorce.

Now she haunts me. I am living in her shadow still. I consider her in my planning, but she's not here. I expect to be seeing her; my whole body expects her, I envision her when I masturbate; her vision has outclassed everyone else.

Now, I can write. It is the only thing for me. I can write while I recuperate, and I can recuperate while I write. I am free to write. Part of me is holding back nevertheless. Part of me is saying that my letter can be reversed, that she can be ripped apart by it or simply sneer at it, and in either case can dismiss it entirely at a later point. Part of me is telling me that I have not heard the last from Rebecca. Part of me, therefore, can't really get into the idea of recuperating, because it's knowing that this is all far from over. I think that part of me is correct.

There was much I ignored. I had ignored that I would not be sitting here overjoyed, but filled with sorrow and grief at losing Rebecca. I am not happily seduced into the half-real world of computer reality, secure in my anchor and free to be sporting about. The computer is a labor to me. I have managed to divert myself with it substantially, but it is not yet my friend, and I don't look forward especially to using it. People say that computers aren't alive, but when they become friends, extensions of oneself, then they have become part of a living thing. Is my right hand alive? It is also an extension of myself.

But I am missing Rebecca. I am watching myself do and say the things that will definitely terminate that relationship and keep it terminated. I am watching, but trying very hard to be looking the other way, terribly uncomfortable that this is going on.

She phoned me yesterday and was trying to get things put back together between us, and I cussed her out for a good ten minutes before I ended the call. I tried to look the other way. I want to get back together. I don't like to see that phone call happening. But it's happening and I'm doing it.

It's simply good overall management. I love her, and want her back on almost any terms, but that's suicidal management. I do understand what I am doing, but here I am, sorrowfully not liking it. I love her so much, but the rest of me says that it can't let me die for love. I love her so much that I want to give up the rest of my life just to have more of her. Bad management. Bad feelings management. Just like Rebecca's problem.

I'm feeling awful and alone. I'm wishing for glimpses of my future, looking there for comfort. I don't even have a clear idea yet of what I want my future to look like. I'm still clinging to Rebecca, even in my efforts at shutting her out. I haven't let go of her.

If I could let go of her, then I could feel free to begin visualizing my future, could feel somewhat confident that I'm again pointed toward my future and not my past. The only attempts I have made at visualizing the future have included Rebecca in some modified form.

No modification seems to work, though, even the very extreme ones. I stayed until closing at Our House last night, really basically unable to push myself into any actual girl-chasing. It just didn't look good enough, tempting enough to me at the time. It looked boring and a nuisance.

But also, I was being very resistant about it. I even wondered if Rebecca used to be among this crowd last year, getting up after we had gone to bed, going out with Mary across the street to Our House, getting picked up or vice versa, turning a few tricks, then coming on back home.

If I had wanted to learn something back then, why didn't I ever take her out to Our House and stand at the bar with her for the evening, and just see how many people came up to her because they knew her? It would never have occurred to me to do that—I had too much proof as it was with the tape recordings, had to quit listening to them because I couldn't stand it anymore. I wasn't about to subject myself to more proof!

And why did I say that to myself? Why did I want to shut myself off from more proof, in effect just bury my head in the sand? Because I so wanted to keep Rebecca. I didn't want to drive myself away. Why would I make such a decision? Shut myself off from a clearer picture of her in order to protect our relationship? Deny knowledge. Why did I deny knowledge? Why does she deny knowledge herself?

I was setting off on the path toward building the kind of family life I knew how to build—the kind I had already built in the past. I didn't stop to question that there might be another way of doing that. I had my teeth gritted because I knew the ordeal that faced me. Develop the sideline businesses. Work, work, work. Save, save, save. And it wasn't what I wanted.

It was taking me right back to the place that required a major escape effort three years ago. I am, of course, realizing all of this as I write it. I have been thinking of how I would phrase a personals ad, though, and have envisioned a lifestyle rooted in poverty, privacy, creativity, and companionship.

I have visualized a relationship with another writer who also requires a lot of time to herself, a serious writer who won't suffer greatly from what are to me reduced living circumstances, and a lovely, sexy, passionate woman in the bargain. But I have been shying away from that vision each time I have put it up because I have felt tugged by my love for Rebecca, by my unwillingness to let her go. I want more of her; I am addicted to her, and the withdrawal pangs are awful. But perhaps I can make the vision more persistent now.

Perhaps I can be more positive about myself now. Perhaps I can forget how little appreciated I was by Rebecca, and remember that many people out there will appreciate me if I give them half a chance to, if I make sure that I furnish a positive view of myself for them to see instead of my dismal outlook of late.

For instance, it's absolutely true that I changed my lifestyle three years ago to become a creative writer. In actual fact, that sentence sums up the last three years. And it's a good, positive statement about me, a statement that may not be welcome news to gold-diggers but then again they ought to be weeded out early anyway.

Looking back, though, I can see how distracted I have been from this knowledge. It is just now occurring to me that I am having to make the financial adjustment of going from work, work, work back to the writer who gets by, who emphasizes his writing over his money-making activities. I got so distracted by Rebecca that I made a number of changes that now have to be unmade.

I can feel my guts shivering right now just thinking about giving up Rebecca for real. I learned a lot about fidelity from dealing with her. And now I need to break that faith. I feel so very, terribly sorry for her. She does love me and need me. And how I need someone to love me and need me! And when she does it right, it is so completely satisfying to me.

She has done it right occasionally. It couldn't have been the real her, come to think of it, because it involved the trust of a child, and trust is something that she doesn't have. Rebecca normally needed me only for immediate relief. She didn't need me beyond the present moment; it was always focused on her needs of the moment. It was often letting her blow off steam about her day at work; sometimes helping her to figure out some puzzling event; often helping her deal with depression; often reassuring her and complimenting her on her looks. Or helping her deal with her friends, her co-workers, her problems with people. Always immediate needs of the moment.

Never working together for what our relationship might blossom into, never sticking to any intentions of getting a book written, seldom enough relaxation to permit spontaneous sex. In fact, she became increasingly uptight about having sex as our relationship went on.

We were both flat-out starved for each other at first, but she cooled rather quickly after just a month or two, and from then on it went slowly downhill. She seldom had any enthusiasm for love-making. She was frequently too tired, or too depressed, or too preoccupied with something else.

She was at other times openly resistant. And there were times when she would give me a sexy lure into the bedroom only to guide the conversation into a hostile attack and an argument.

I enjoyed her sexually all the same, but I missed her participation. She just did as she was told, like a whore, though I usually paid attention to her preferences. Jill used to tell me how much she enjoyed going down on me. I liked that a lot. I would really have liked hearing that from Rebecca.

I created a vision and fell in love with it, a vision that Rebecca fulfilled for me. I owe her. But it was my vision. If only she had loved me enough to really be my whore, to be the free and willing sex partner I wanted. She started out that way, but then it ended. I wonder if, under the present circumstances, she would do it again? I wonder if I, my events manager, would let me take her up on it?

I'd sure think about it. I'd be up for that one. But, God, it would be so dangerous for me. It could suck me right back into a relationship with her. Maybe my events manager can be told to switch away from work, work, work. No, I guess that's not what's behind what it's doing. It's my survival as an artist that's being protected. I gave up my ambitions of being a writer for Rebecca. It was an agonizing price at the time I did it, but I loved her that much.

And now, here I am, on September 22nd, in front of the finest computer I could have chosen for myself, equipped with the latest technology to help me be a writer. Sitting on my curious new computer chair, at a desk, in a bright and airy private room just for the purpose. A writer's heaven. Except that I am alone here, and I sense that as an unnatural condition as urgently as the pressure in the vacuum it is pointing to. Tautological perhaps, but hey I'm talking about a feeling.

I hate my job.

So, when do I, and how do I, make that final and absolute decision to abandon Rebecca. I just don't think I can ever trust her, even if she had a panel of psychiatrists tell me that she is now a single, integrated personality. None of her personalities was really trustworthy to begin with. If you can't trust, you can't be trusted. I don't think integration would give her anything new that she doesn't have now. And I'll never love her fully again if I am unable to trust her.

I simply and truly do not want a woman who is not going to be faithful to me, sexually and emotionally. Her condition is very severe, and there is probably very little chance that she will ever be an integrated person. Which means that if our relationship continued, my time would be constantly consumed with dealing with her problems. And not with writing. And my feelings would be again in constant turmoil. And I would again be extremely tense and inefficient. And I would again conclude that it is too much. Too much energy, too much sacrifice, too much agony, too much misery.

But how do I let go with my feelings? This talk is okay, but it's all talk. What do I do about the fact that I love her, that my heart is broken because of her? How do I fix that up? It seems like it would help so much to have a woman especially for the purpose of comfort and consolation during this period. Someone temporary, sort of like a combination of nurse and surrogate mother and wife.

I am stoned. I just got high on Thai weed, and then did four or five hits of hash. I am being all uptight and trying not because I am taking tomorrow off (a Friday) and so my weekend has begun already and it is time to stop being uptight.

I am uptight because Rebecca left me a message yesterday on the answering machine saying she'd call me tonight between six and six-thirty; and I have been thinking about that phone call all day. I have been rehearsing conversations with her all day.

And that tug of war has begun again, with the opponent tugging me into making love with her again. I am trying to figure out how to make it happen without having to make any commitments. And I fantasize about how wonderful it will be. And the little nags get to gnawing, poking AIDS at me, poking the danger of getting hooked on her again at me, poking the danger of too soon forming a new and happy relationship with someone new at me.

We can begin to establish a new relationship, I am pretending to say to Rebecca, by being lovers. That's where most of your problems are rooted, anyway, so it will be a good place to pay special attention. And we will confine our relationship just to being lovers, for a stage.

And she will sweetly acquiesce. Happily ever after. Sure. Because I know Rebecca, that is indeed a fantasy.

It is 5:10 now. In about an hour, she will call. She's calling to arrange to pick up her file box and some clothing. Tomorrow sometime, her day off, and I am taking it off, too. And I say to myself, hmm, I wonder what that will lead to. I know I am so stoned because I was afraid of her phone call. And am. Because I don't yet know what I'm going to say. I'm not feeling markedly angry at her and I've been saving up a lot of chastity for somebody.

Yes, I still love her. I don't feel that I need her anymore, but I love her. At least, I was feeling that before I got high, as I was walking home from the T. I'm talking about the need part. Right now, an hour or so later, I am feeling needy. I want to fuck her! It is her last hold over me. She has that sublime pussy. The immovable stalwart meets the irresistible temptation.

I want to be all right. I want to go to work with the understanding that the best thing I can do is to do my job well. And return home, sit at my console and write wonderfully. I want to feel good about the time I spend awake. I don't want to feel like I am hiding from everyone when I am at work. I don't want to feel like Rebecca is breathing over my shoulder as I sit here and write. I want to be alone and all right with myself.

I don't want to be haunted by Rebecca. I want to be naturally me, comfortable with myself, unconcerned about playing roles—that friendly, lovable, laid-back champion natural person that I've glimpsed in myself. I want to strip away all the shit that stands between that natural me and where I find myself to be. Dealing with Rebecca won't cut it.

Where I find myself to be is where Rebecca put me, to a large extent. I even now wonder if that is really true. Before that, I was rather crazy. Crazy metaphysician. She put me through a lot of changes, and I grew. She was so good for me that way.

But my guts have been screaming, enough is enough, I can't take any more. She set out to destroy me, and ended up taking a lot longer at the task than she had anticipated. She had met a genuine challenge, and she took it up. She knows. She doesn't forget experiences and things, she knows.

Multiple personality is her best mask, her best protective device, but just a thin bit behind the mask, she knows. And it's right there for her. She knows, and invokes the mask to hide behind so she won't give away the fact that she knows. She knows it all. And she set out to destroy me. She damn near did it, too. She had me sliced up badly and left for dead, emotionally.

I'm doing some acid Saturday night. I haven't stopped to think about why, but I sense a lot of activity going on with me about it, and it's what's happening. I've been staying high all the time I'm not at work for a few weeks now. At work, my day bums me out. I show up with some residual high and feel fine, often able to actually do some work. Then it wears off and I become anxious to leave the office, and I go for walks or to the smoking room a lot. I think I need a good shake-up so I can let go of my anxieties and begin living again.

It's twenty before six, and despite my little lecture to myself, I am still feeling her phone call in my crotch. The one time she was here in my new apartment, she could only do oral sex because she had had a cyst suctioned or something and was still healing. She not only chewed me up good by scraping her teeth on my dick, she immediately inspected her damage when she was done. It seemed deliberate.

I've been trying to analyze Rebecca's phone message, her tone. She was very quiet, even cowed, said she would call to "negotiate" picking up her things, stuttered on the word "tomorrow." I suppose she was feeling very uncertain of where she stands with me at the moment. She apparently did not take my farewell very seriously.

So you're still angry, that was her reaction to my cussing her out at length on our last phone call. She didn't hear what I said, she just picked up the anger. Same with my letter. So she'll probably start out the same way this time. And I'll probably be gruff and make the phone call brief to buy myself some more time, until she gets here tomorrow or whatever.

But what if I say that I have the day off tomorrow and she says something about coming early in the day and so on and so on? I'll give in to it, I know I will. And then what?

It's seven before six already. I don't have much more time to prepare for this phone call. I'm still caught in

124

the middle between knowing the best thing for myself and giving in to irresistible temptation. Maybe if I give in just a little, or just for a while, just until I get situated in a new relationship or something. Just a taste for now, maybe. God, I am starved for her pussy. It's not good for me to be without a lover. The phone is ringing.

I told her right off that I have the day off tomorrow. All she had to do was ask what a good time would be for me. I told her. But it didn't make much difference. She then said Trisha was coming over, too, and that she needed to check with her also, and then call me back at nine tomorrow morning. So it looks like she was scared that I had taken the day off, and quickly decided that Trisha was going to accompany her. Or if not scared, she may have thought that I took the day off for her, and saw an opportunity to strike me. I guess that's the more likely.

I showed myself. I volunteered the information and showed my hand. It was bad gamesmanship on my part. I hadn't even considered how she might receive it and multiply it into something else.

But I did make the phone call brief. I was disappointed when she said that Trisha was coming, and she must know me well enough to have picked up on that, too. That volunteering of information about my day off either cost me some good love-making, or it saved my ass, depending on how I want to look at it.

So she already called and she'll call me again at nine in the morning. And she'll either offer an excuse for Trisha, or Trisha will come. I had better sound mad; I gave her too much hope tonight. She thinks she still has hooks in me. Which she does, but I have to fake it to her perfectly like she doesn't.

So, am I going to be on my toes enough to remember to watch what it is she's doing? To figure out what is being aimed at me and why? To step aside when the deadly blow is struck? I don't really appreciate the seriousness of my situation; my cock is really in the way. I probably won't be on my toes. And I'll probably be high.

I am visualizing fighting with her. Putting my hand over her mouth while she is giving me a final all-out striking angry tirade. She biting my hand, me summoning my intense concentration for a mighty and sudden jolt downward with my hand to harm her jaw, she being injured and throwing something at me, me grabbing her arm and twisting it behind her, putting my free arm around her throat.

Do I want to kill her? Not with Trisha watching. But if we were alone? No, her absence would be investigated. If I could really get off scot-free and never even be asked about her? No. I'd make her my slave instead. I'd hog-tie her to the bedposts. I'd keep her in a cage. I'd beat her. If I could do it without any fear whatever that I would ever be questioned about it? That's what I'd do. I'd remove her teeth so she couldn't chew up my dick any more. I'd put her head in a brace and fuck her throat. I'd dominate her.

It seems I'm reacting to her domination over me.

It occurred to me to look for my pictures of Rebecca nude. I found them, and looked through a pile of others in the process, seeing Rebecca at various points in the relationship. I took the picture of her lying in bed wearing the red snap-crotch lingerie thing I bought her for our wedding. It was the only time she wore it. It is a beautiful picture; she looks radiantly loving. It is the best of the wedding pictures, I think, for me, anyway. It shows some of her pubic hair. It is much nicer than the picture I took of her pussy.

God, how I yearn for her body, her sweet loving. The picture makes her skin look pure white, and it's not, of course. It has patches of mottling, stretch marks, varicose veins, several things that I paid little attention to because the body was marvelous in spite of these flaws.

I relate best to her body. It never really changed very much from day to day, the way the rest of her did. It was a constant that I could cling to, not like her various personalities and never knowing which to expect or when. If she were a normal loving wife in that body, the way she seemed to be for a time, she would still be my wife.

She was made for sex. Perhaps her early head start is responsible for that. God, I miss her, I miss making love with her. I hope to God I can find someone else that good. I wonder if a person has to be crazy to be that good at love-making. Probably not, but it's certainly rare. Or is it? Was it the pot that made the sex seem so good? What about those less satisfying nights when I wasn't high? But, oh, those wonderful nights when she fell asleep under me, and I continued intercourse for as long as I could before I was exhausted. It was heavenly. Being high helped those out, too, but I'd never had that experience before.

She was so happy to get married to me. She didn't fully believe it was happening. She was a perfect bride, practically blushing. I didn't take it as any big, serious thing. It was what she wanted, it didn't make that much difference to me whether or not I was married to her, and so I married her. I would have preferred to remain single with her, but it was so important to her, getting married. And I didn't want to lose her.

But I never even got her. She got me. I got dominated. And so I got out.

But what a wonder she was! I look at the picture, and I remember how happy we were to be going to bed together, how filled with anticipation we were, how hungry for each other we were, how much we loved each other. Absolutely wonderful! Life's best! I could think of nothing more in the world that I wanted. I was totally happy. My whole world was filled with Rebecca, especially making love with Rebecca. I couldn't wait to get home to her when I was at work. I was happy and cheerful at work, spoke with people, got friendly, because I was high on Rebecca.

I was so proud of her, and proud that she was mine. But I didn't feel comfortable talking with her when she phoned me at work; somehow, it was violating that private world of ours by mixing it up with the work scene. I never spoke of her much when things were going well; it was only when our real troubles began that I began speaking of her, in need of sharing the immense burden. I kept her private. She was my treasure, and I didn't want her to leak out into the world. Which, alas, turned out to be her nature.

Earlier this evening, I was remembering Leslie, how we used to kid around together and really have fun doing it. We were very compatible people in terms of ordinary getting along. I haven't been as comfortable with a person since. Not Jack, not my son Hector, not Jill. Not Rebecca.

Very seldom did I feel acceptable to Rebecca. Sometimes, but not often. Or is that true? Am I just being bitter? I do think she found me acceptable. It's the others who didn't, and who let me know about it. The one who found me acceptable adored me. She got drowned out. All because I represented too much of a threat to them. They destroyed the sweetest part of Rebecca so they could get at me.

By the time I had identified my enemies, I had been weakened too much to fight them. Is that true? When did I identify them as my enemies? I had identified the striker early on. It is only occurring to me right this minute that I had no idea that Rebecca herself was actually vulnerable to their attack, that she could be killed off. I believe the thought occurred to me at some point, but I quickly dismissed it as nonsense. It was one of those impulsive thoughts that is automatically screened out.

It shouldn't have been; I missed the whole ball game because I screened out that thought. It is only occurring to me right now that after my Rebecca had been killed off, all that remained were my enemies. All that was left of Rebecca was enemy others, and they were all aiming at me. I am only now identifying the enemy that clearly, and the fight seems to be over. Or, I have been weakened too much.

I am in the process of springing back. It is like swimming in molasses. I want to be sprung back, but I have a ton of adjustments to make in the process, and it's dreary work. I am being selective about who I want to be; my list is drawn from that laid-back natural me that lurks within. But so far I am tensed almost all of the time, up tight.

I need to relax. To think how much study and practice I devoted to the art of relaxation, and now I can't get relaxed enough to relax. I still feel under attack from Rebecca. I interpret everything about her phone call as attack. I am wondering what she is going to do next, trying to figure out her strategy. I haven't been very good at figuring out her strategy.

What I end up figuring out is what my own strategy would be, and hers turns out to be mystifyingly different. And I have gotten better at spotting it. Or more paranoid about her. No, I think I am spotting it. But since the separation, I have only the phone calls to go by, aside from the one visit which was after just one week, and the rest of the time I speculate on what she might be up to.

I fear her at the same time that I worry about her. It is extremely painful to me to think that she is miserable. It is so painful that I try not to think of it at all. But I know. And I know that my Rebecca is not there, that the enemy others have the pain to themselves. They are wailing, trapped in a person with no forefront for them to hide behind.

I look at the picture. How wonderful she was. And how horrible she has become. She really did get sucked into the love and the relationship for a while, just like I did. For a time, she seldom attacked me. The attacks came in sudden spurts, like lightning striking, leaving me speechless and breathless. It was so disorienting that I could only be struck dumb by it. I couldn't take a second to stop and figure it out. It was horrible every time.

The worst attack was when she told me about sleeping with my brother. I still don't know if she made that story up or not. It would have done its damage either way. It was as if the occasional attack was testing my weak spots, checking me out. How horrible she has become. Is that true? I want to make love with her this minute. But her driving force, how evil it is, how cunning and destructive. Making love is fine, usually, but any other kind of dealing engages the enemies. I want her as my lover, I do. That's all, though. And I can't see her going for that at all.

And that's progress to look at, now that it's right in front of me. All I want of her is to be my lover. I used to want everything. I have let go of a lot with regard to Rebecca. With a good new lover, I can let go of that one, too.

I handled it masterfully. I went down and opened the front door for her, and we talked about the problem with the door buzzer. I led her into the apartment, headed straight for the bedroom where her bags were, and I handed her the two small things and told her I would take the big one down. She said, "Oh, okay," with a touch of surprise. We talked very little and didn't waste a moment.

I don't believe we had any direct eye contact. I studied her fanny as we walked, though, and decided that it wasn't so hot, ass-wise. I scanned her, not daring to look directly enough to establish contact. We put the things into Amy's car, I said hi to Trisha and Amy, wished them a happy hurricane, and turned to walk back to the apartment. Rebecca called thank you, and without turning around completely I said, sure. I went in the building; they drove off. I felt pangs of sorrow, regrets, and I shut them off. I had to. I still had the stairs to climb.

I didn't give in to temptation, though. She didn't especially try to be irresistible, and that helped. We both kept our distance from each other. She was wearing blue jeans and a top, a sweater, I think. I didn't really notice. I noticed her short hair, though, which startled me a little bit because I have been remembering the better times when her hair was long.

And I have been looking at the picture, where her hair is long, permed and gorgeous.

I always gave her her way. I always let her make the choices, the little decisions, because I wanted her to be happy, and I had reached the point where a great many things had become immaterial to me. A while back, I would have asked her to figure out how we should carry today's bags down to the car. Today, I was masterful; I simply told her how it was going to be. And she was a little surprised.

I wasn't falling apart at the seams. I was looking and doing well, self-sufficient, in fact, and in no need of Rebecca. I can't tell if she was surprised that I had offered to help her carry the bags, or that I was being in control, or both. But I hope she saw that she no longer dominates me.

She was quiet today, polite, subdued. Her only words with any emotional content were thank you, voluntary words on her part, not needed to transact the business. They were a reaching out, the only words that reached out to me. I gave her no such words at all. And she reached out, a little. It's difficult to evaluate. Was it simply a residual reaching out that she couldn't stifle? Which would mean that the relationship is over in her mind. Or, was it the best she could do given her current personality? In which case, there is more interaction to expect. And increased difficulty letting go for me.

Since she was walking in alone, I asked, hopefully, Trisha didn't come?" And Rebecca told me that Trisha was waiting in the car with Amy. I stepped down on my anger. She had used the very same device once again on me, giving me the illusion she was alone and then interjecting Trisha into the picture.

But Rebecca wanted the opportunity to be alone; else, Trisha would have come in to help carry, and instead she was waiting in the car. If Rebecca hadn't used the word waiting, like say she had said, "Trisha and Amy are in the car," I wouldn't have pounced down so hard on my hope that we had an opportunity to be alone together. But the word waiting made it sound somewhat urgent, and that's what hit me.

She must have wondered about, and anticipated at least somewhat, the possibility that we would make love. Part of her loves to make love with me. Or, used to. Maybe that was part of the Rebecca that isn't there anymore.

On the phone this morning, she told me she missed work yesterday because she slipped in the shower and gave herself a concussion. She's trying to kill herself; they are trying to kill off the body, because they can't stand being in there without the forefront Rebecca to hide behind. Or maybe they are punishing her for letting me get away undestroyed.

Wednesday, two days ago, my phone rang once at 4:20. It would have been about the time she got home from work. She was making a phone call first thing, and dialed my number by mistake. So she must have been thinking that day about calling me. She had told me she would call on Wednesday or Thursday. Wednesday would have seemed eager, she may have thought.

I didn't touch her today, not even accidentally.

She must have gotten a glance into the kitchen and living room, and then was in the bedroom, and saw a reasonably neat apartment. Maybe that, too, was part of her surprise. I was dressed neatly, have an almost fresh hair styling, and looked full of energy. And acted it, not extremely so, but I wasn't being slow about what I was doing.

She must have sized it all up, and felt very left out, felt that this was an alien environment to her. It was all very distant to her. But her last words were kind, a reaching out. It will be a nice way to remember her. I left her with much less. I am still angry, and behaving so.

I look at her picture, and that note swells into the symphonies I used to feel part of when we made love. It is wonderful to have such memories. I'm remembering how I used to give her front rubs, and how I got to ending them up with clawing, mock clawing from her throat to her pubis, clawing that wasn't really clawing except when her nipples got clawed. I assumed that hurt, and I liked hurting her just a little bit like that, and she always enjoyed it. And how I would go down on her. And she would clutch my head and force my mouth against her, sometimes causing me to cut my lip but it was always exciting.

In the latter phases of our relationship, she stopped being that rough with me, because I had complained about my lips getting cut.

And how she screamed. My God, she screamed her head off, five or six prolonged yells, writhing all over the bed all the while, as she came over and over. I can't believe I adjusted to that screaming, but I did. It was electric to me, once I got over my concern that other people might hear her. It went through me like a sexual shiver. It was a sexual shiver, exactly. Over and over. And I couldn't wait to fuck her, hoping greatly that she had a good pussy tonight. Sometimes she did, sometimes she didn't.

It's almost noon, and Hurricane Gloria is supposed to arrive around noon, getting serious this afternoon. I wonder how it will change things for people? and for me?

I am lucky as hell, you know that? I'm sitting here with my wonderful new computer, watching my printer produce perfect pages of type. The stereo is playing in the background. I had bacon, eggs and toast and coffee for breakfast after sleeping in. I have the week off. I'm high. I have a recliner to sit in, and not a bad apartment. I have friends. They are strange kinds of people to me, but they are friends. Michael is a friend. Linda is a friend. Donna is a friend. I have friends.

I have a good job, which I had better get around to preserving. I've been extremely weak at the job for many weeks. But in spite of that, I am a very lucky fellow. I mean, just look at me now. I'm a writer in Boston doing okay. Free to do whatever I want to do. Free to be me.

I am free of Rebecca, by virtue of my assertiveness. I still yearn for her, still think of her often, still argue with myself about shutting her out of my life. These feelings are in my heart, though, and I don't want to snuff them out. These are my own feelings, and I want to preserve them because they are mine. I haven't had access to my own feelings for 20 years. Rebecca made it possible for me to fed again. I'm still learning how to do it. So I don't want to shut out the feelings I have for Rebecca, because I owe her for them.

God, when she was wonderful, she was so extravagantly wonderful! But she was equally hurtful at other times, times that I barely survived. What a wife she would be if she were always wonderful. I drool at the thought.

I'm also free to reclaim memory of my life. Reclaim having experienced my various roles. Assemble all of that stuff together so that I'm completely the life I have lived. That, along with my constantly increasing knowledge of myself, should sit me up pretty.

I was rereading Castaneda's *The Fire Within,* reading the description of a warrior, suddenly understanding at long last the concept of aloneness as it applies to a warrior. I suddenly felt very positive about the aloneness that had been a real problem for me since the separation.

It meant that I was free to be myself. That there were no real other people looking over my shoulder, nor imaginary. That all I needed was to have clear objectives, and a strategy for each. That intent is available to me as a power, and assigns much of the responsibility for strategy to the unconscious.

Free to be me, free to live the life I want. I wanted to fuck Rebecca. Just make love with her, not get involved with her problems again. Love her with all of my heart and make love with her. Just that. All I had to do was make it a clear objective, and then intend it, and then monitor and cooperate with its unfolding. It was simple.

There were no moral or social standards involved. There was only what I wanted most in my life at that moment. It was a pure desire, uninfluenced by any oughts or shoulds. And good overall strategy required that any encounter be limited to loving and making love.

That was Friday night, October 4th. The next morning, I phoned her and was very mild-mannered. She wanted to see me. I knew that because she was making an exaggerated issue of returning the photo albums to me, for safe-keeping. I resisted the suggestion that we get together, as a matter of cooperating with my strategy, and held as firmly as I could without sacrificing the ability to take an opening when I finally gave in.

Her plea changed to an urgent, critical need to see me to discuss our termination arrangements, that it couldn't wait, it had to be done right now. She wanted to see me, bad. So since her objective was basically the same as mine, all I had to do was ease it along.

She came over early that afternoon with the photo albums, and we talked about terminating our relationship. After a lot of this, I suggested we look through the albums together. I got romantic about the memories, more strategy and some easing along, and when we got to a photo of her in bed, I commented on how very precious my memories of our love-making were, how I thought we were absolutely fantastic lovers, how I had never encountered such a woman before in my life.

Then we went on to other photos, and after a while I stuck in something similar again, and she shared that I am the only one who has ever brought her to orgasm. I was easing it right along, but there was a lot of space to cover, since this was our first meeting after a very stony few weeks of silence.

Once she got to the point of saying that she could foresee us sleeping together at some time in the future, it was only a matter of minutes before she modified it to the near future, then to days, and then to that evening if I would go home with her. Which I gladly did.

Going home with her was strange behavior for me. Only one day before, I would have strongly resisted going, insisting on my turf. But strategy made it clear that I needed to cooperate with its unfolding by going to her apartment. She was jumping on her tiptoes with her hands clapped when she invited me, saying "Pretty please?" I was delighted, not only with the invitation and her excitement, but over the rapid accomplishment of my objective.

Our mutual objective.

She treated me like a very special guest, making sure I was comfortable, that I had tea, and so on. So I kicked back and relaxed. I liked the apartment. We went to bed, and she was feeling shy and self-conscious. She didn't know if she would be fully comfortable with me. But she was. I went down on that succulent pussy and worked it up very slowly, and she exploded over and over, screaming and shouting at the top of her lungs. When I fucked her, she was overly moist, and didn't feel tight, but it was good, and I came hard in her. And then she propped her head up on pillows and I fucked her mouth. And that was absolutely sublime because she kept her tongue resting against the underside of my dick the entire time, and it felt maxed out the whole time. I was slow because she wasn't fading out at all, and I was easy; I didn't do any sudden shoves or anything. And when I came, I screamed, it must have been for fifteen seconds. I don't remember for sure. It really knocked me out.

Sunday night, we came to my apartment. She wasn't as relaxed. She doesn't seem to feel at home here. Anyway, she turned into a cunt bitchy mouth and we made love but it wasn't especially great. She had a nice pussy that night, though. Snug.

We made a date for Friday. Tuesday, she called me at work and invited me to come to her place after work. She said she couldn't wait until Friday. I went home first, packed a bag, and went.

When she showered, I snooped in every nook of her apartment. We made love very sweetly that night. Our fucking was very good. She went down on me, but with less patience. Amy came home a short while after we had finished making love.

Friday, she came to my apartment and her conversation broadly wandered to termination, and gradually became more and more specific until it was clear that she wasn't going to see me again. She didn't know if she loved me, or if that was some of her others who have died off. The sane Rebecca I spoke with that first Saturday was nowhere to be seen. She said we could make love anyway, but she was completely unresponsive. It was a good opportunity for a long, slow fuck, and I fucked up my come by trying to make the fucking last longer when I had to come. But it was very good all the same. I had given her a long back rub, and had gone down on her bum and her pussy, and finally she just stopped me. So we fucked.

It's a private experience for me when Rebecca's not there in it with me. It's different from sharing the experience, but it too is very pleasing.

I phoned her yesterday and talked for an hour, but she was still in the same mindset. Although, there was a small opportunity for me to offer to visit her at her apartment, with the understanding that she couldn't make love with me. I didn't have the heart to push it, which means that I'm not tending to my strategy, and in view of that I think I will call her again. I am willing to bet that all we need is to be alone in her apartment and that she will steer things around to making love.

I was slipping back into aspects of the relationship that I had intended to delimit. It was a good test, brief, a toe-dip into the water, just enough to try myself out, get what I wanted, and get out before I got burned. But I have been missing her so much since I saw her last. I remember that she gave me almost exactly the same rap once before, because it is in this journal, and I know that I only have to wait for her to slip into another mode before I can be lovers with her again, but I fell in love with her again last week, and I am having separation pangs all over again.

They are nowhere near as extreme as before. I am dealing with them okay, but I am constantly a little tense, and am aware that I am dealing with them. I'm not feeling free from having to deal with anything. Somehow, my strategy will have to include devising a way for me to fall out of love with Rebecca as quickly as I fall in love with her, just so I can have some peace in between. She does it, of course, but I don't want to do it her way.

Making love that Saturday night was so special. It had been so long since we had made love, something like three weeks. We were both as sweet as possible, both so grateful for each other. It was sheer bliss to be in bed together and making love. She was glowing in the way that makes her extremely beautiful. And she has lost weight so that her body was the slender one I remembered when we first met. Everything was perfect for us that night.

But now, after that week of Rebecca, I am not the clear-headed person I was a week ago Friday night. I am not clear about my objectives. I have Rebecca watching me over my shoulder again. She makes a difference to me again. I need to get back to that clarity that had me working happily on the job, that had me being open and friendly with people.

I was thinking that maybe LSD had given me that the weekend before; and that somehow it might have taken it away again last weekend. I need to not need, to behave in accordance with objectives and strategies rather than emotional tugs and pushes. It was a very clear spot, that Friday night. My mind felt washed and rinsed, clean and fresh, unencumbered with irrelevant garbage, and who I was within this life seemed crystal clear.

I am an artist at living, alone in the world until and unless some bonds of intimacy form, free to create whatever reality I want for myself, and able. That Friday, the reality I wanted to create was very clear, Rebecca. But this week, I don't know what my objectives are, not with that kind of clarity. I have the usual confused desires for sex, but they are not phrased in terms of particular objectives. I don't know what kind of woman I want for certain.

I look at the picture of Rebecca on the wall in front of me. That is the woman I want. That's the problem. I want that woman with the terrifically sexy body. I already know what my chances are of finding another like her. Something like one in a hundred. God, I catch myself licking my lips when I look at the hair sticking out of the crotch of that red nightie. She's definitely not fair to other women.

I called Rebecca this morning with the objective of arranging to make love with her. She was ready to suggest that we have a meeting, but that it be limited to conversation. I told her we could do that over the phone, started pushing her with the idea that I was going to find a new relationship, and said goodbye.

A while later, I impulsively called back. I had just toked up. I told her that I couldn't leave things that way, that I loved her, that she should call me for a visit tomorrow when she's in the neighborhood. She said she was leaving for the neighborhood in five minutes because of a change of plans, and would bring her own tea bag.

Between the two phone calls, I had fallen for the idea that it was over. I had forgotten that I had stated an objective and that strategy had begun. It kept on going even if I had lost faith in the project. It's scary to think about. Past objectives still unfolding in my path. And it makes me timid to formulate objectives, at least before I am fully behind them myself.

Maybe if desire fades away, then the process fades away. Maybe my desire didn't fade away, just my faith. (I haven't admitted to having faith in decades!)

I am sensing the onset of a personal crisis reaction, so I decided what the hell, it's 5:10 on a Saturday, I have nothing to do for the rest of the weekend, hey, it's a good time to let it happen and get it over. So I just toked up and dropped two tabs to help things out a little.

It's Rebecca, of course. I called her yesterday, and she told me about how she's going with this Egyptian guy now, tried to make it sound all nice and nice like she wasn't just out there getting fucked, but it's screwball anyway. It hurt. I sort of nudged her into saying that she had made the final discovery and decision that she no longer loves me. She told me not to keep my life on hold for her. When I said I'm not, she made me repeat it and sobbed, tried to muffle it. It hurt her, too.

I told her that in a way I was glad she had finally made her decision about me, since at least it told me that I really was free now, which is good to know. But as I was saying it, part of me knew very well that I have not let go of the hope that she will be around some more, that I have not fucked the last of her. And it's still possible. But of course, I do have to utilize my freedom, and point myself forward again. I do have to think of her only as pussy from now on, pussy that I may or may not have from time to time.

I really haven't managed to remember why it's wonderful to live alone. Maybe that's an accommodation I used to be able to make, but that was before Rebecca. Since Rebecca, I have no desire at all to live alone. A normal amount of what Rebecca overwhelmed me with must be very satisfying to have. Reaching and touching an intimate lover without having it turn into a nightmare, that must be fun. Being lost in love with someone who is lost in love with me, without having it torn up by sudden crash landings, that must be great. Thinking ahead to the future together, that must be fun with someone who can do it for real because she has faith in me and wants what I want. Having a lover make love with me freely and eagerly because she loves me and loves love-making, it must be fun to be that way ordinarily instead of once in a while mixed in with hostility, depression, illness, and outright total rejection. I don't

143

want to live alone.

It's 7:15 and the LSD is starting to hit me, I am having a few shivers and am feeling anxious. I am sort of floating in and out of where I am here. My hands look like foreign objects on the keyboard, but only somewhat so. I have a slight tremble. I am taking an occasional deep breath to calm myself. This is the first time I have done acid alone, and I thought about that but decided that I was safe enough. I haven't lost very much control before, nor experienced anything really wild or cosmically unreal. I am remembering that I wanted to cry, that's what started this piece of writing, it's why I did the acid. But I'm just a little apprehensive all the same.

I'm supposed to be working at home today, and I haven't been able to get started. Part of me is anxious to wrap things up here and take off. Part of me is depressed. I'm out of dope as of yesterday; I'm supposed to get some tonight, some hash and a sheet of tabs, and I hope that works out.

I was up until three Tuesday night with Mike and Darlene, doing acid and laughing, and it has me tired out. I haven't slept much more than three or four hours a night for the last many nights. Nor have I been eating regularly, just averaging a meal a day. It's been raining yesterday and today, and that bums me out, too. I think of going back to El Paso. El Paso would have sunshine.

I still feel wounded by my relationship with Rebecca. There's nothing to do in this apartment, and there's nothing to do outside, either. I'm far from being where

I want to be in my head. I want to be happy and cheerful and fun and exuberant and humorous and exciting. All I am is bummed out.

God, how I miss those wonderful days when Rebecca and I were in love. It was the relationship that marijuana made possible. I couldn't have endured her for very long without pot. Nor could I have examined myself closely as I did and learned about myself as I did without pot.

How glorious it was to be in love, to be needed, to have expert love-making, to have a secure love-nest, to be high, to have good music in the background. I could have stayed lost in that forever and considered myself fulfilled. It was as good as my life has ever been.

I don't think I'll be happy again until I find that kind of experience again.

Last night, I met two interesting people. One was Link, a very mellow, warm, fun person. And Christina, a 14-year-old hard-ass, cute, vulgar, violent, and so extremely into her character that she is a non-stop amazement. I like her.

I've finally done coke, free-basing mostly and some snorting. Tuesday night, there was a super coke party, about seven or so of us, and there was about 16 grams around, more than we could use up. I didn't get off on it Tuesday, but Wednesday night Mike scraped up some of the resin and I got a rush off of that, but no big deal.

145

I have two days of work left on my current contract, and then I am adrift for a while. I don't know if I am going to Texas or not.

Right now, Mike and Darlene and Valdez and Christina are all in the living room, playing with my Model 100 computer. I've meditated, washed the dishes, sat with them a while, and now am in the back room. I haven't the slightest idea what I want to do this evening, except I want to take it easy, get straight, get rested, and get ready for an all-out weekend.

I've been high much of the time I've been awake lately. I haven't been writing much. I've been hanging out with Mike, and Mike has been hanging out with me. It's been a lot of fun.

I am thinking that my life is very confusing right now. It has many new elements in it that are not frightening me the way it seems they should. Dealing drugs for real, seems like that should be frightening. Dealing with Rebecca coming back, that should be frightening. Dealing with visiting Cindy in El Paso, that ought to be frightening. Dealing with the possibility of being out of a job, that ought to frighten me. Being high much of the time and forgetting what it's like to be straight, isn't that frightening? No. Taking a deliberate vacation from my writing, is that frightening? No, I just miss it. Free-basing cocaine, what about that? Not frightening. The only frightening thing I can think of is Ben in a paranoiac attack, swirling and crouched, scurrying and furtive. That was a little scary.

I dabble with the fucking inner unknown with very little fear. I suppose on the outside I may have developed a sense of what truly is fearsome, and can see that quite little out there is actually fearsome.

I am collecting many precious views of life and many life experiences that are new to me, and I know that I will want to write about this period of my life and of the people in it. Yet, I haven't started making notes. Like when Ben put the tab in his mouth and then asked, "What I do, man?" because he didn't know what to do next. And how he resisted swallowing it because it was a piece of paper.

We have attained cruising altitude and the fasten seat belts sign has gone off and it is okay now to turn on my computer. It has been a wonderful weekend in El Paso with Cindy. A wicked weekend for her, a delightful weekend for both of us.

I am up in the altitude, heading for Albuquerque and Denver. She misses me already, and I miss her. Neither of us knows what we are doing with each other. We are completely mismatched in so many ways that she thinks are important, and in several ways important to me. It's altitude. We both wanted some altitude, and we got together for a weekend and lost ourselves into each other. We got altitude, we got high on each other. We ate lavishly, we fucked and sucked endlessly, we climbed the rocks and looked at the mountains. We talked. Mostly, I talked.

It's the only adventure I have for you this time, I said. And it's not really that great of an adventure, but it's a good one for you. The last adventure I gave her included champagne which was liquor for her first time; sex with another man, me; giving head, the only time she has ever; seeing Niagara Falls; touring in my Mark V; lots of adventures for her. This time I offered lavish eating and marijuana, but she wouldn't do the smoke. It shocked her but she was mostly amused by my smoking.

She sort of made me quit smoking cigarettes for the weekend, which I did okay. She told me that our last weekend together, three years ago, that's how long it's been since we've seen each other, was the best time of her life. Then a week or two ago she called me out of the blue. She was divorced for six months now, and she was lonely. I am the only other man in her life, so she called me. And I dashed off 2400 miles across the country to see her.

So what is that? Anyway, she said that our weekend together three years ago had been the best time of her life. She never sent me the letter that said so. Instead, it got misplaced until her husband found it a few months later, and he never stopped using it, couldn't stand the idea that the best time she had ever had had been with me.

She has the body of my dream woman, petite and perfect. Her pussy has blossomed into a fleshy flower, and she has real pubic hair now. She was fully cooperative in having sex with me, and even came when I went down on her this morning. Very encouraging improvements in her attitudes toward sex. And she has a good pussy, tight and lavishly oily. She tastes of that delicate sweet nectar like that Susan who I just got a lick of once before she got timid and quit.

Cindy said she didn't know why she had called me, except that she was lonely. She didn't know if she wanted to see me. She was worried that she might be interrupting a relationship I might have. She hadn't decided to have sex with me, so she said, right up until we did it, or at least until she asked me if I had herpes or AIDS.

Her thoughts simply do not keep up with the events she wants and creates at deeper levels. Friday night, she complained about her pussy being sore, after I had eaten her out and fucked her. But Saturday night and Sunday morning, there was no mention of soreness. There was only her desire for more sex.

She kept me in bed this morning for more sex. And we screwed twice and I ate her until she came. It felt very good to make her come like that. It was a controlled come, with only a certain amount of moaning, but I'm sure she thought she was exhibiting an extravagant sexual response. She must have thought she was loud. She really thought I was loud.

I fucked her in several different positions, because I was sure they were all new to her. She ate it all up. She didn't go down on me, and told me ahead of time she wouldn't. She is intrigued that I really love going down on her. I think over time she will take on that adventure, too, with seriousness.

She is a closet adventurer, and I am her only source of adventure. It is strange being the only man in her life other than her husband. It is strange that there is this woman 2400 miles away who thinks of me, loves me, wants me, yet is frightened to death of me and can't conceive how we could ever live together, especially with her son at home. Perhaps in eight years, she said. She wouldn't want to expose her son to me, bad influence. But she wants to expose herself to me, same reason. She soaks up my bad influence, at her own rate of course. But it will gain speed.

She is such a cute little piece. She still looks 21 and that's not stretching anything. She doesn't even have wrinkles under her eyes. As Michael says, she doesn't even have breath yet. She is as innocent and pure as she can be, given that she has been married. And she'd rather not be. And I love her. I told her, I love you, Cindy, but I haven't the slightest idea what to do with you. She agreed, has the same feeling. If it were just her, minus her son, minus her family, minus her church network, she would let go and hang in there with me. I know she would. It would be the grandest adventure of her life.

Cindy said she has never had anyone in her life with whom she could share her feelings honestly without fear of being preached at and generally rejected. She still didn't reveal very much about herself, but some things gradually came out. I don't know what they were, now.

She only gave me a few decent kisses. She thought maybe my beard annoyed her. I suggested that I shave off around my lips and laughed, and she said her husband had done so and it did look silly, and so he shaved off the rest of his beard.

Rebecca has managed, so far, to be consistent in keeping a loving attitude toward me, which is what I told her I had to see in order to believe. But I feel like I am dealing with a desperate and needy personality that is doing its dog best to please me, and that there is no one else there.

150

I feel like I am sleeping with a whore, an extremely life-like inflatable doll that I could probably do anything I wanted with since we have been doing more and more than we ever did before, almost all at her instigation.

I do cherish and enjoy her; she is dear to me. I'd hate to live without her, without seeing her regularly, and I'd hate for her to live without me as long as she loves me and needs me so intensely. But I am becoming more and more detached from her as a person. I know that I am not dealing with a real person. She has described the couch she sleeps on as if I had no knowledge of it, when it is a couch we shared for a year. She laughed as if for the first time at the Attack Cat sign in a storefront.

She is very different sexually. She conies during intercourse now, almost continuously, and they are her complete bloody murder screamers. She suggested the doggie position, which she would never agree to before, because she had a tummy ache, she said. Last night she was crab-walking for me, spontaneously, she said. I haven't had a good, quiet fuck with her yet. They've all been adventures. It's as if she is trying very hard to be my whore, the best whore possible. That's what I want from her. But I can't believe we'd agree to that in out-loud words.

It's winter. The sun doesn't shine. It's cold out. There's some snow on the ground. I feel half-dead.

I think of Cindy. Rebecca studied her picture and said she looks like such an innocent. Lynda is taking me to the festival of lights or

151

something tonight, says it's metaphysical. Rebecca will wait for me here. She's here for the weekend. And I think of Cindy.

My joints ache, and I think of El Paso. The sky is dreary and I think of El Paso. The days are short and I think of El Paso. An occasional sandstorm is nothing, nothing. And I think of Cindy.

The sun is shining on her photograph, framed and on the wall above my desk. Her hair is very different and it is a studio pose, not really the Cindy I saw recently. But the photo reminds me of what she actually looks like, and I can see her clearly in my mind.

She commented that we spend a lot of our time together in a car. It is a land of symbol for us. Perhaps we are vacation partners. I keep having the idea that we should meet at Disney World in January.

Dear Rebecca,

This is the anniversary of our meeting, and of our wedding. We have known one another for two years now. It is like a day, and it is like forever. Two years is a small part of a lifetime, but you are without doubt the most important person I have met in terms of a relationship that has benefitted me and my personal growth. And you are also the most fascinating person I have ever met. Unfortunately, you are the most difficult person I have ever met, and you present a serious challenge to me.

I love you and care very much about you, but from just enough of a distance to avoid getting hurt myself.

This means that I am there; if you can see beyond that small distance you will see that I am there. Don't let the distance frighten you and make you imagine horrible things.

There is so much that I cannot do for you that I wish I could do. There are things you must do for yourself. Please believe that I am always using my most considered and thoughtful judgment when I do try to do something helpful. I apologize for my failures, but please see the concern and love that is behind them. And I encourage you always to tackle your problems with your fear under control.

Happy anniversary of our meeting. I wouldn't have missed meeting you for the world.

Happy anniversary of our wedding. We can never see the future, but we now can see a little of our past. We had a rocky first year. Next year will come and go a day at a time. Let's influence those days and make them good ones.

My hand holds your hand.

Just had a talk with Rebecca. She was desperately trying to figure out how to kill herself. So, in talking, I formed a new concept about her condition. That a personality is actually a memory receiving an overdose of attention. There is something wrong in the system that directs the attention. My current understanding is that the unconscious operates the attention, specifically that part of it that I call the events manager.

My life seems so haphazard, so unprotected. I am prepared to die, am on the ready moment by moment, wondering what this business of going with the flow of life is going to force me to collide with. I feel too lucky so far, wondering when I'm going to land on my face. And behind me is my other mentality saying that it's all cool, just fucking relax will I.

Ordinary reality itself has become superficial to me. There is nothing left in it to really take seriously. It is not of enough consequence to foster any care about it from me. It has become reduced to my kettle of fish, my pool of resources for survival and pleasure.

I miss reality. I think about it and cry. Hazel the rabbit died and made me cry today. There are no longer women to love, only female things on the prowl. I don't want them to touch me. My body has minor sex urges once in a while, but nothing like the way it used to be. My eyes still want to look, and I have to avert them which my anger makes easy for me to do, or else I return hard stares, uncaring see-through-you stares. I walk like get out of my way. And yet my habits make me smile like a nice guy when the chick next to me asks if that's my bag and I say it depends on what's in it which is half a sandwich. I haven't much practice at being not Mr. Nice guy.

I'm really upset about discovering that love with a woman is an illusion in the service of repopulation. That responsibility for repopulation makes women maintain control of the planet and of men. That is a bald and patent fact, clearly observable just as soon

154

as one is willing to see it. And my grief is immense; it is the grief for every love I have ever had.

I wanted my mother's love, but it was reserved by my father. He was openly sexual with her in front of us, always grabbing her and handling her, and that taught me how to gain the love of a woman, I suppose. Somewhere I learned that sex was where it was really at. Except that now it's not.

But what is this prolonged walkaroundangry thing about? This hatewomen'sguts thing? You're not facing things the way they are. It is your illusion that has been burst, not anyone else's. So you want to take it out on women? Why not figure out why it is the way it is? Why not line up a few of your ducks?

Why kiss off Cindy? You know very well that a day may well come when you'll want her. Why make it so tough for Lynda? Why shut Rebecca off cold? Well, okay on Rebecca. And why not turn on Ladybird? Or Vicki? They're hovering all over you. It would take you all day to get married to any of them.

And trade the illusion for the reality. The reality is good to know, but it's no place to spend a lot of time. So get back into the illusion and tuck your secret knowledge away for a while. Write your novels and plays and stories. Become wealthy and famous. Enjoy the illusion; none of it has taste without the illusion. Leave the reality behind, or better, find ways of working it in, as you write.

I know you can do all the right motions and not have a bit of fun out of it. Do things for fun, for pleasure, joy, satisfaction. Taste what life is like at each step of the way. Your mission is to enjoy. Don't drive yourself crazy achieving; that will come by itself. The opportunity of living a life on earth is rare, and you must not waste yours, and you must encourage others not to waste theirs.

I'm feeling more up since getting prescriptions from Dr. Wills yesterday for my throat and my inflamed wrists and hands. But I'm not back to work on the job yet. With only two weeks to go before my contract runs out, I'm not really inspired to buckle down. There seems to be a chance that my contract will be renewed, which would present me with a real dilemma. I want to quit so badly. But I'm not very secure, and the money is really quite good, especially since my living expenses are down now and I could save most of it. I know I will be unhappier choosing to continue working. I know I will survive somehow if I quit. The question is, which way will my novel get written faster? Will I be spending most of my time hustling money for staying alive if I quit, and have no time left to write? Will I be better off doing the novel spare time and keep the good bucks rolling in? I don't know how to think about it. Prudence pulls me in one direction, and strong desires in another, the desires to be free, unemployed, unencumbered, free to be me, free to be only a writer. Free to be a character. Free, simply free. And lost, lost in freedom, with only my writing to anchor me. No more anchoring to people; let the parade pass on by. Alone and free, alone, miserable, and free.

It's not easy to think about. I have been slow but sure productive while working in misery at my job, and that is something, that is accomplishing some real writing. I don't know if I would write more if I weren't working. And I don't know if I can handle the freedom without going berserk. But then I'm going berserk on my job anyway. It's not easy to think about.

Structure for my Alfred T. novel keeps feeding into my mind, and I have quite a few ideas to consider. It is clear at this point that this will be a monumental task for me to complete. It will keep me alive, I hope.

I've been depressed, by grief, for a long time now, a couple of months or so it seems, starting with the last contact with Rebecca, the last being-together contact. I was so relieved to see her go, and then I was depressed about it. And then my illusions about Cindy disintegrated, leaving me feeling very sad and broken, very depressed. I turned to Lynda, and was rejected without explanation.

That just plunged me deeper. It's been a very difficult time for me, the weather has been miserable both in terms of having to live in it as well as how it wracks my body with arthritis, I've been feeling suicidal at times and really consistently shitty the rest of the time. I've got to quit my job if only to give myself a chance to feel good, even if I do blow it.

"It's over, I hate you, goodbye," Miseral said.

"Yes dear, I understand, I'll always be here for you," Alfred T. said.

It was the macho thing to do, the manly thing. Certainly this situation called for manliness? Manly in the face of this suffering woman, this anguished woman who seemingly by accident has ripped out the heart of Alfred T?

This woman who was failed by Alfred T, whose expectations from her man were so woefully underachieved, who had no choice but to break off the relationship—and just look at the piteous position she had been put in by Alfred T.

He had to be manly. He had to embrace the surge of heartbreak that welled up in him, threatened to explode him, stripped him bare of his face in the world and of his happiness and joy at being alive; he embraced it to push it back into himself, which required all of his weight and muscle. He had to be a man Miseral could count on. He couldn't show his feelings; except that there was only blue.

He could smile for several weeks, though blue, until the blues overtook him and the smiles became very forced.

The blues grew until he went crazy. Something snapped, and he was able to laugh again; but he had lost heart, he was not as warm a person now, there was a cold edge to him that had sharpened itself on heart flesh.

He would love again and the coldness would seem to vanish; but heartbroken once again his edge would sharpen more, and gradually he was becoming a dangerous man. A day would come when he would explode, and he would be a danger to the woman who triggered it.

A parade of slut pussy modeled fashions by Boston designers in a slapdash and fucked up midnight revue at Our House last night.

The program was emceed by a fat bitch blackass from a radio station. Men also modeled.

I sat in there and bitch women fucked with me. The prima donna running the show wouldn't get the fuck out of my face and ended up shouting an insult at me and walking away. Some blonde bitch behind me began interrogating me and I tried my best to tell her to fuck off but she was thick and it took a few exchanges. And the black pussy who modeled wouldn't quit checking me out so I told her a bunch of shit and she went away.

Pussy. Walk in front of me, give me a look or two, make it clear to me that you have a pussy there. It's all you are.

It's all you are. Cunt. Your currency in life is cunt. You expect to get everything in life with just your cunts. Put some crazy clothes on your cunt and walk on by. If the cunt smells good with those clothes on then you've got a good design, a design that might get you something, a date, a relationship, an annuity. Jewelry, trips, drugs. Dress up your cunts so they can pull in the best you can get. No wonder cunts smell like fish; they are fishing, all the time, for whatever they can get.

If I put a computerized cunt on my machine, I'd have the perfect woman, keyboard controlled. No sleaze cunts fucking with me trying to do my life for me.

I don't even know why I was there. There was lots of cunt around, but it leaves me cold, cold fish cold. There was no exceptional person there. It was a population of homogenized cunt, all looking for dick. I'm not dick. I think I'm looking, but mostly I'm eliminating what I see because it's not what I'm looking for, though I wonder what I am looking for.

Not just eliminating—I'm slashing at what I see because it is so completely not what I am looking for that I don't want it in my face.

I am so alone, and so angry at being alone. It's a very cruel position to be in, and I don't deserve it. And it will take more than a patchwork solution to stand me back up. I want to spray a grandstand full of women with an Uzi and see who is left standing when I'm done. Somehow there must be an exceptional woman out there, and there must be a way of recognizing her.

No, the concepts are too glaring when seen naked, they are overpowering me, I have seen too much of the inner workings of reality and it is like looking at raw viscera oozing and pulsating, it is not a pretty sight, reality really sucks at the level of concepts which underlie this maya illusion material world concept. It is far better as well as more to the purpose of life to remain lost in the illusion; except that this harsh knowledge of the nature of reality must be preserved, and its tenders, the seekers who carve for themselves the niches of keeper of the burning flame, the searing torch of knowledge, the disillusioning clarity of vision, they are the sacrificial lambs, giving themselves for the preservation of truth in the world.

The path has been deceitful. It has peeled opened my eyes, and my brain is on fire with horror, in anguish. I know more than I can bear to know. It is ricocheting through my consciousness like St. Elmo's fire, dancing impossibly crazy dances, driving me berserk, driving me into a sustained freak-out.

But today I began considering the idea of having a girlfriend. It still sounds like a suck idea, but at least I am thinking about it. It's a suck idea, but it's the level of illusion I have to get back to if I'm going to get out of this futile mind trap I've been in for the past few months. In and out of kind of in.

What about that laid back nice guy I was talking about some months back, the one in me I thought I wanted to have out front as my usual self? He got attacked so bad so often that he fucking retreated totally. Now it's no more Mr. nice guy, it's me the sonofabitch. I wonder if I will again find myself in a relationship which I trust enough to enable me to be nice? I really want to be nice, so much, but it's gotten stepped on so fucking much, so bad, that it drives me fucking crazy with pain and horror. Women are so fucking bad, so cruel, so like a stiletto with its own mind. Relationships now begin as a contest to see who can kill the other first, I suppose.

It's so hard to believe that there is a woman out there for me, one who is really suitable. Yes, I am still wanting her, now that I am beginning to peek past my pain a little bit. But I've become so confused about what she would be like. I suppose she's petite. And very beautiful. Where do I go from there? Is she smart? I suppose so, but maybe not. Is she into her own thing? I'd prefer that I were her own thing, that she got into me. Is she young? I think so, perhaps extremely young, but perhaps not young at all. I don't know.

I am thinking that I ought not light up for every woman I see, as I have done in the past. I should be flat out rejecting of any woman who doesn't meet what I know of my description of my companion. I have nothing to lose from being hostile to such women. I suppose I need not attack them wildly, but I can certainly attack them enough.

Waitresses always try to be friendly; they want a tip. Men fall for it, thinking there is some real feeling there. That's the kind of thing that I can be intolerant of, that I can attack. "Madam, I do not require a friend, only satisfactory service." I don't need you, that's the gist of it. I don't need you. That's all I have to do, make it plain that I don't need you. Realize that I really don't need them, not all of them, almost none of them in fact, just one. And every one of them is absolutely not a candidate, and there is almost no risk of attacking the one by mistake. Women as women get attacked. I can deal with them as people; but not when they start getting female.

Nor should I be desperate about finding a companion. The fact is that there are zillions of scum sluts to go through in search of the one. The one will probably have been raised by a man. So I need to become an expert at cutting women down. I need a lot of lines at hand. I've been working on that.

My poor mother, she didn't know she was doing it, but she taught all four of us boys not to lie, and it was so that we would be the more controllable by women in the future because unlike the women we men would have a strongly developed sense of guilt about lying. The same emphasis on honesty is not given to girls.

We have to discard that sense of guilt, and adopt dishonesty as a frankly useful and important tool in human relations.

Life has really seemed, lately, not worth continuing with. I've avoided meditation lately, and I suspect it's because of the temptation to just take off and stay there. I don't want that to happen unless I fully agree with it. Part of me holds back, whispering that there's an end to this, that life can be as good again as it is now bad. Part of me whispers, the rest of me shouts back, Aw shut the fuck up, what the fuck do you know? But I have been a real madman lately, way out of control, very hostile in my attitude, very arrogant and pushy, out playing in the traffic.

I am going bananas. I am on a three-day weekend, and this is Saturday night and I'm having real trouble getting myself out of the house. I don't think I'm going to manage it. It's so pointless, anyway. Go out spend money on beer get drunk feel like shit come back home. Something lacking there. I want one dove in my hands, and the rest of the world can go fuck itself. One dove in my hands, looking at me softly and cooing. That is a large enough illusion for me.

Being my woman is a tall order, and I'll have to help someone to do it, which means I need someone who will learn to do it. A child, I think. Someone who hasn't yet learned something else. This idea is getting serious.

It is rolling wonder, tumbling surprise, and it is another day in my life. There is nothing there, and there is a sudden gasp of encounter with meaning and what it means makes me cry and turn away. It is drawing out the sting and it is sucking my blood. It is today.

It is looking at now, and all day went by before there was any now. Bruising from every gentle touch, too hurt to trust a light caress. It is knowing that this is not the way for it to be, and knowing that it will be this way tomorrow. It is today on the grin of death.

It is conjuring events and then fearing them because they are within reality. It is fearing reality, thinking reality is more than the mind that knows it. God, what an ever-present fear.

Which is this little girl,
which is she? She who cries,
or she who laughs at me?

Is she wanton and depraved?
Does she cuckold me?
Or does she fold into my arms
and dedicate herself to me?

Is she some two-minded freak?
Or is it all a play for me?

What are all these tell-tale signs?
how am I to conclude?
Is she hiding much from me?
Or is she out of touch?

How can she stroke me and caress,
and love me as her only best?
And loving, exit as a beast
rampaging through a sexual feast?

Why would she beg me for my love,
my promise that I'll stay

if then she turns to everyone
degrading all I am?

Which is this little girl,
which is she?
The little girl crying?
Or she who laughs at me?

I have been working hard training people in word processing, working hard at developing my buyers coop business, and reading, and generally living a somewhat tense but ordinary life. I have been quite successful at filtering out any perception of Rebecca's outside sex activities, and we have been happy about half of the time.

But last night it came up. She has been overtired, often sick, hostile toward Linda who may be collaborating at night, as she was toward Mary last year, and in the routine of asking me how I slept after we had discussed the significance of the question in the past. It came up, and I am obsessed by it, once again. Yes, the clues are there, I've been filtering them out but now I see them. Last night she said she thinks she must be going out at night again, or still.

She said things about Mrs. Hyde that I hadn't heard before, things I wonder how she knows. She said Mrs. Hyde tells people that this split personality business is just a cover story she tells to George to keep him strung along, that she's actually a very promiscuous woman. When she told the story about Joe who telephoned, she added to the story by saying he had said that she sucked his cock in a car. It raises my suspicions about just how much she does know, does remember.

I'm obsessed by it because it disorients me completely and I feel a desperate need to reorient myself. It depresses me because I feel hurt and angry. Top that with: insulted, aggrieved, degraded, maligned, abused, abused, abused.

My only refuge is my computer. And some smoke.

Yet, I can't permit myself to become intimidated by my reactions. I'm not going to go through another prolonged stretch of high anxiety. I'm either going to deal it swiftly and effectively, or insistently filter it all out again. Up until yesterday, I did a very good job of filtering out the clues, finding a face value explanation and dismissing them. It has worked for me, well enough anyway. But it leaves me too lopsided to filter out that large an area of my life. I need to come up with a better way of dealing with it.

It is very difficult to love her blindly if I see. I enjoy loving her blindly very much, but perhaps I should love her with my eyes open. And find some way of dealing with the pain. Perhaps find someone with a love I can trust, so that I can feel loved even if not by Rebecca. It's odd to me to approach a problem on the basis of feelings.

I think her dominant personality is Mrs. Hyde, there's the true Rebecca. Mrs. Hyde, manager of the total person, including my wife. She is the personality with the most drive, the most energy to expend. She uses the energy and leaves the other personalities exhausted. This normal person Rebecca business is an act. It has no depth to it. Mrs. Hyde has depth. This I can see when my eyes are open, when I am not filtering things out.

166

I can no longer pretend that I know her. I am just beginning to see her as she is. I would need to study her intensively before I could know her, as well as objectively. I already know a lot, but it is just so many scattered pieces of a puzzle. I don't have an idea of the whole picture yet.

He can make it real in his mind, she realized. He can actually imagine it so completely that he is able to enjoy it, and it's all in his mind. He really can do it.

When I am high, I am brilliant. My mind is released from the constraints I keep it under, and it soars. It is free to be creative and perceptive, free to think very wonderful and grandiose things, and I get into it so much that I realize that here is my real mind, this is what my mind is really capable of, if only I could dare to turn it loose. I come to remember that this free mind is who I really am, and that means that I am seldom in touch with my true mind.

And I am high, with my mind soaring ahead of me, luring me into my future, wanting to give me the reins, and it feels like taking a first step felt.

My soaring mind, so far today, has yanked me into my business future by making me see the aptness of the situation for successful news coverage through a mass mailing of news kits to editors. It costed out to $2222.20. And it seems right, barely affordable in the near future, urging me along. It will catapult the business and seems to be a smart investment. My ordinary mind hadn't been open to the idea, it shunted aside the possibility. It took a contact like this with my freed-up mind to enable me to think it out very quickly.

Was toying with the idea of developing a John Kelly character to play, wondering if I dared learn the South Boston accent.

Rebecca has been having a very difficult time for several weeks, becoming totally stressed out from the load of her job plus starting to figure out her disorganization. I am so pleased to see her confronting herself and committing herself to her rehabilitation that I rather overlook the serious struggle it is for her to get her pieces back into place again. And she feels that I don't care enough for her.

She is my greatest treasure, the most wonderful thing that has ever been in my life. And I've made some progress at handling her attempts to strike me down. And I love her.

I feel my skin is being ripped off my body by the sheer speed with which I am hurtling naked through space; not now, but at a moment when I anticipate rising above my current level of consciousness and into, perhaps, my truer self, that conscious state I remember where everything is clear, just as if one

168

could see one's life being played out on a miniature stage at one's feet.

That anticipation shows me that in the process of rising into something I also have to rise out of something, something that has to be literally stripped away from me, because it has allure I can't resist.

I have been occupying myself overly fully for several weeks. As if I didn't want to have time to stop and think, like avoiding something I'm supposed to be thinking about. I'm still waiting to come into myself. I'm still holding back, holding up my guard. I'm not sold yet. I'm waiting to get rich first.

Then I can be silly when I want to, outrageous if I want to, entertaining and fun.

I've been smoking pot of late, regularly now for a few weeks. I am beginning to feel too dragged out by going to work to manage to get my list of errands done. Of course the weather has been dreary. But I am no longer as clear-minded at work as I remember having been before. My clear-mindedness has been exhausted by getting my mail order gig up and running. I've been feeling half-awake in the mornings, when I was much brighter before.

Sheila is the one I would call the manager. She makes the shopping lists, sorts the cupboards. She is about sixteen. Her handwriting matches those on her letters to me, her husband; it is the handwriting of the one I can identify as the all-business Rebecca.

She is bright and capable, but has limited experience and is very unsure of herself. Much of her conversation is filled with assertions of her competence. She retains firm control of the situation.

When I'm high, my imagination and intuition are really opened up and I can tune in to some very interesting concepts. I can "recognize" which Rebecca is being identified, given a set of clues. The above are my first flush of data derived from clues.

Here is what Rebecca wrote while I was writing the above:

Sheila-Strong, courageous person. Strong sense of self purpose, conscience, values. Stubborn like a mule about opinions, beliefs, concepts, yet can be open-minded when occasion calls for it.

Resorts to her own counsel while carefully weighing others. Constrains emotions, feelings, keeps them under tight wraps, yet can break constraint when necessary. Works as back-up reinforcement for Marla. Sheila is ageless in sense she has always been there since the tragic events occurred. Always given responsibilities well beyond years with firm expectation from others to fulfill them. Came out strong and steady at age 16—manager halfway house where lived.

There, now that we have satisfied that little rush of urgency about getting those words down, please allow me to become more organized.

My own fear has kept me blinded to the necessity of writing about what is happening with Rebecca. I have suddenly had a release of that fear, and I am exclaiming to myself: You fool! This is all happening right fucking now and you're a writer and it's all yours! Start writing!

The fear was so awful that I am surprised that it is gone.

The story of Rebecca is a story of unimaginable complexity, only some of which I have figured out myself so far. I am married to a woman who has multiple personalities, eleven of them, so far.

As a writer, I've been feeling intimidated as hell by this story. At this moment, my story is starting to slip out of my fingers because the things that are bound to be the major things seem very much to be happening right now, and I'm not taking notes, nor do I have time now for notes. I must produce final copy as I go.

This document has just taken over my journal, which for a few years now has been focused on my life with Rebecca. It will continue to be my journal, my personal record of what we are going through now and how it is upsetting our lives and how we are managing to hold things together after a fashion. But as of now I am writing it for you, and I'll try to have that in mind all along.

I assure you it is a story that is happening right now, as I sit in my little office upstairs at my computer, as Rebecca is getting dinner ready for company that won't show, two friends at the hospital where she works who called a little while ago and cancelled.

So, it's... Rebecca fixing a special dinner for us, linguini with white clam sauce, I bought some really far-out looking pastry on the way home, so there's dessert.

On June 3rd, Rebecca wrote the following. The first is a handwritten note to her psychiatrist.

Dear Dr....

Enclosed you will find list of names with personality traits.

While housecleaning today I happened to be looking in a mirror as I was cleaning it—instead of seeing my reflection I saw these people inside of me. I took a piece of paper and pencil and let them/someone write down the list with characteristics accompanying names. Something like being emptied out of yourself, feeling your hand move and write but knowing someone else is doing it.

Don't know how else to describe it. I hope you find it helpful, for both of us.

Sincerely,
R. Lareau

The list of personalities with traits is hand printed:

172

Mrs. Hyde: hates men—> prick tease sexually—> indiscriminately active, involved (hates children) bisexual preferences—> both men & women

Marla: supervisor referee—> pseudo therapist, parent/caretaker loves children/loves life, likes people

Marlene: cynical nasty, short temper sarcastic hates in general contains lg amt rage, murderous hate anti-social

nobody: no name no identity reclusive—> fears people, hates people

Jennifer Moore: 10 yrs old innocence of childhood immature, childish fairly pleasant curious about things in general

Becka: 8 yrs old suicidal very withdrawn, quiet keeps to herself hates, fears people, contact, closeness

Becky: 4 yrs - 2 yrs varies in her age between 4 - 2? quiet, fearful, frightened, afraid

Bette Davis: young woman likes men, likes fucking

Mr. Hyde: violent explosive, homicidal anger & rage hates children

George's wife: devoted & domestic good lover, companion, friend

As we were discussing this list that day, we were speculating about where the characters might have originated. She then wrote the following (hand printed):

"Mrs. Hyde: literary character ? from book

173

*Marla: Marlo Thomas "That Girl" series, role model, name Marlo too harsh, Marla more feminine

*Marlene: Marlene Dietrich actress

*nobody: denial mechanism in character form

*Becka: character from book "Little Princess" main character suffered much loss abandonment, etc. worked out in the end. Becka childhood name from siblings

*Becky: origin of self

*Bette Davis: Movie star Bette Davis role model

*Mr. Hyde: Father's violent monster incorporated within

George's wife: Mother's role model with father as young woman and mother.

And then yesterday she came up with three more (longhand):

Mary: approximately 21 years old quick wit, good sense of humor comes out at particularly stressful times or moments

(Mary Tyler Moore show—sit-com)

Marion: (Marion—> Robin Hood's lover/mistress) approximately 12 years old mild stuttering at times, with very low self esteem, deeply troubled & insecure, unsure of herself, little confidence difficulty initiating, easily intimidated very shy, sensitive, introverted difficulty socializing or relating to others

Book work—lives in her head and fantasies, thinks

she is ugly and unattractive craves warmth and affection yet fears closeness good student intelligent capable of falling into semi-acute catatonic or withdrawn states

Rebecca told me that right after she had written about Mary and Marion, it "came to her" that Sheila had written that. We both went to work seeing what we could find out about Sheila, me by seeing what clues the writing contained and she by gathering impressions. We ended up with two different perspectives, but they both seemed to me to be describing the same person.

Rebecca's account was quoted above. Later she added this:

"Sheila: strong, courageous person with strong sense of self (real or imagined?), purpose, conscience & values. Stubborn like a mule about her opinions, beliefs, values/concepts yet can be open-minded when occasion calls for it. Resorts to her own counsel while carefully weighing others. Carefully constrains emotions/feelings, keeps them under tight wraps yet can break restraint when necessary. Works as back-up reinforcement for Marla.

Sheila is ageless in origin in sense she has always been there to some degree since tragic events took place. Came into her own with full identity and name at age 16 yrs when Rebecca was in a halfway house for drug & alcohol abuse as resident receiving Rx. Took name Sheila from former resident who struck her as her own person type of independent woman.

175

Always given responsibilities beyond her years with full expectation from others to competently fulfill them.

Yesterday, Rebecca said, "We've forgotten about Prudence."

I said, "Who the hell is Prudence?"

She described Prudence to me, and yesterday I spent the day, most of it, with Prudence. Prudence is a teenager, a devout Catholic who wears a pained long-suffering expression when I tease her sexually. She is quiet and serious. Prudence lives in fear of violating rules, is dependent and shy. She fell into place immediately since I have spent many, many of my days with Prudence in the past two and a half years. I just never knew her name before now. Nor did I realize she was a separate personality.

They've all been Rebecca to me. Just like I do with anyone else I know, I attributed traits and behaviors to only one person.

It makes such a difference to finally have this list of personalities because it organizes the reality of Rebecca in a way that I can relate to. Before this list, she was a chaotic and confusing person to me, often extremely frustrating for me to deal with.

With the list I finally have a way of understanding her that is organized. Organization is very important to me in my concepts about things. Organization contributes heavily to my understandings of things. I feel lost without organization, and that's how I felt with Rebecca until these past two weeks.

The list is completely acceptable to me because it fits, as in those beautiful cases where theories fit the facts exactly. The list may not be true, but it certainly gives the appearance of being completely workable. I can recognize these personalities; they are people I know, except for Mary who apparently comes out when Rebecca is at work. She works as a nursing assistant on the medical/psychiatric floor of a hospital.

But I know the others. I've made love, talked things over, fought, been viciously attacked, been seduced, been cuckolded, been used and abused, by various of these personalities. The spectrum has been broad and extremely erratic, and it has been absolutely confounding for me to attempt to incorporate all of these behaviors into my concept of one person. No concept has been large enough to contain Rebecca, until the lists came along.

Before the lists, we talked about multiple personality. To me, it was one of those labels that I had no experience of, and I talked about it like I talk about lots of things I don't know about, things that have been given labels and attributes and a certain dimension of clichés called common knowledge, but it was nothing my experience in life had prepared me for.

I could try to apply the idea that Rebecca had multiple personalities, but it didn't help. She was still erratic and confusing to me, completely unpredictable, impossible to understand. All I could do was love her, be patient with her (which took a lot of growth and learning on my part), and keep on struggling for understanding.

The lists make all the difference in the world to me. Now I can say to myself, well, this is Prudence or this is Becka, and I can observe the behavior and see that it conforms to such and such a personality, and then I know who I am dealing with (well not yet, I still have to study the lists and become more expert at identifying which personality has the stage).

It makes a big difference, because now I only have to deal with them one at a time; I have a way of telling who I'm dealing with, and I have a way of understanding the characteristics of the one I'm dealing with.

It's going to seem—for real, now, though I've used the expression before—as if I'm living with more than a dozen women. That's exciting to me. I can manage that, and it provides a fascinating life for me.

I think that the story of me is just as important as the story of Rebecca because I've had to cope with her using all of the means at my disposal, including some that I have to call extraordinary. I've been driven nearly mad at times, I've experienced the worst depressions of my life at times, and I've also experienced the most sublime moments of my life which has been the cement that has prevented me from forsaking her altogether (which I did once though we reconciled after seven months).

I will call her Pandora. I have to change her name, after all. Pandora was the first mortal woman sent by the Greek god Zeus to punish mankind for the theft of fire by Prometheus. When she opened the box which Zeus had given her, Pandora unleashed all human ills into the world.

My Pandora has not unleashed all human ills upon me, nor has she abstained from bestowing many wonderful times upon me, but the name more or less fits. There is also the sexual pun on the word "box" which is appropriate because Pandora's multiple personality problem seems to stem directly from sexual abuse. And I like the idea of deriving a name from the Greeks, a people whose ancient wisdom has yet to be completely rediscovered. I've needed to tap into any wisdom available, from whatever source, in my long attempt to understand and cope with Pandora.

Later:

Don't think all I do is sit here and write about this. I am teaching word processing full-time, managing a mail order business start up which involves a surprisingly large amount of work or did until very recently, and I have a typesetting customer who publishes a small newspaper. In addition to this, I am a writer and I do manage to continue writing on a limited but fairly regular schedule. It is on top of these things and others that I am now beginning to write what is bound to be my major opus.

I can't say the timing is good; you know the old saying, give it to a busy man if you want it to get done. But really, I had envisioned myself with leather slippers on, sitting in my recliner, smoking my pipe, my cocker spaniel at my feet, when it came time to do my most serious writing.

I am high now, in case you can't tell. It has taken me the last three years to train myself to write with sustained coherence while high. I'm still feeling insecure about it, but I seem to be doing it well enough a paragraph at a time.

Now I'd like to train myself to keep my thoughts sustained. My writing creates the illusion that I can do it, but in fact my mind flies off in five directions for each phrase I write. My mind is in toy land, delighted by the overwhelming array of attractive concepts afloat there, and sparking with revelation each time it

179

can make new connections between concepts, or add a new track to a current concept.

It is working its switchboard frantically to keep up with all of the connections that have been identified as simultaneously workable, and as soon as I have a phrase in mind ready to type, it flies off and does several other things while my fingers are busy at the keyboard.

I am an extremely fast typist, and it is sobering to see my typing speed as the thing that is holding up my flow of thoughts because it is so slow by comparison.

Sometimes it takes several moments to attract my attention back to what I am writing. Sometimes it thinks that it is doing more important things, that my writing can wait another several seconds, and then I get impatient and remind it who is in charge here. And that's my practice for learning to sustain my attention, I suppose.

Although, this business of being able to freely access what seems to be an endless storehouse of ideas and concepts and to make, actually create, new connections and new relationships between them, that is nothing I really want to give up, now that I look at it. That is too damned much fun. It is a creative gourmet feast.

Yet, my sense of discipline—funny I should write that, because I usually refer to myself as undisciplined while I am actually quite a highly disciplined person—sets the next challenge for me. I don't know the reward of it; the labor of it I can guess at.

You will see that I am fascinated by my mind, how it works, what its powers really are. It has been a lifelong and ever-present challenge to me. People with self-centered minds have always piqued my immediate interest. They seemed to contain new mysteries for me to learn.

My interest in my mind began early in my life. I apparently had a concussion from a sliding accident at about age four. I recently tapped into the memory of what I experienced then, the safe space I was in, the warmth of everything, the timelessness of it all. And then the voices reached me, a crowd of relatives surrounding me, my eyes opened. With a memory like that in my mind, whether I covered it up until my age 45 or not, I had something feeding my curiosity.

I was a physically and emotionally abused child, along with my brothers; I was the oldest of four boys. Being raised like that fucks up your mind. I lived without a clear concept of who I am for most of my life. I studied acting in college, and I played roles in life. Seasonally, the play changed; my seasons ran about three years at which time I brought about some major changes in my life, reorienting it as completely as possible.

This seems like madness, a mad way to live. It is a madness fed by one's search for oneself, a driving passion for that primal possession that permits a person to know who he is.

I am not telling you about my mind accidentally, by the way. You need to know the ins and outs of my mind if you are going to be able to understand the story about Pandora. This story is being told in the language of my mind. That is why I want to show you a lot of my mind, so you can understand the language.

I do believe that my mind is different from the minds of most people. I mean, I know I am intelligent, some kind of flaming genius, but that never satisfied me—I always wanted to be the top dog, the smartest man in the world.

But it is possible that my mind actually did change from experiences like daily two-hour meditation for fifteen years and at another time the use of drugs, along with the fact that I learned dozens of ways of making a living. Maybe like playing the Megabucks I have hit on a lucky combination of things and my mind is the big winner.

Let's face it, my mind fascinates me because it is my mind. And the minds of others fascinate me because they help me understand my own.

There's a great deal of mental anguish that goes along with being an abused child. I was told daily for years that I was a bum, and that I will always be a bum. It was in no uncertain terms, either. And it was during the years that I was a young child, putting together my pieces for understanding myself, my life, and the world I was in.

Now, I know that I am not the only child who was ever abused. I was surrounded by them in school. It was like a sign of the times, places I lived. What I am saying is that the consequences of it are still real. I suffered those consequences; they had a very major impact on my life. They shaped and affected my mind. Correcting that situation has been a real bitch for me. Most of the changes happened to me after I met Pandora.

Those changes are interwoven into this story and into my mind, the mind that is telling this story. Where I'm going from here is no longer anybody's guess. From here on, I know who I am, what I am doing, why, and I'm making sure that I'm having fun.

Even I am somewhat apprehensive about poring through those thousand pages, reading what my mind has been through, digging out enough of the good stuff to lay before you and in the process being reminded of it all. I haven't read those pages but once since I wrote them.

I realize how polite I am being with you. I am on my best behavior, as I am whenever I first meet someone. This will change, though, as I get to know you—and I will. As I write and you read, I know what is going through your mind because I wrote the words. After a while, I will know that you know enough so I can trust you more, and I'll become more plain. Perhaps not to your taste, I will become more vulgar. But hey, that's the kind of guy I am.

I've been searching for Pandora's mind since we met, on Christmas Day of 1983.

Generally speaking, men can tune into concepts much more readily than women. But they seldom can do anything more than tune into them by themselves; they usually form bands to collect pools of energy to activate them. Men can dream the grandest dreams and they will too often remain only dreams.

Generally speaking, women can tune into energy much more readily than men. Their recognizably more noticeable expenditures of energy as emotions reveals them to be great channels of energy.

But on their own they seldom tune in to their energy creatively and it is wasted. Lately, they have been turning to men's organizations in search of concepts to fulfill.

As a still current general pattern, however, women seek people who can give them a concept they will enjoy and they energize it. It is a perfect combination, and accounts for many marriages and successes.

Only concepts can be energized. They are mere ideas without energy amplifying them. The right team of a man and a woman can harmonize as an energized concept, the one fulfilling the other, and have the impact of a corporation of men.

Energizing concepts materializes them. With energy, the concepts become strong enough to begin emerging into reality, and they grow or die, as is typical in nature, in this case depending on how much benevolent intervention is provided in their behalf by their caretakers.

I'm real scared to write about her, man. I'm writing bullshit, telling myself how important it is, so I won't have to be writing about her. But I've got to do it.

On the night of our first date, a number of Pandora's personalities paraded themselves before me. I think they all wanted a peek at me for themselves.

I had no idea at all that it was occurring, of course. I mean, I had not been eagerly waiting to meet my first multiple personality, nor did I wonder about every woman I saw: Gee, I wonder if she's a multiple personality? It really wasn't on my mind, nor in it.

But this is two-and-a-half years later and now I can look back and see them, each one, standing there bold as fucking brass.

When I opened the door, she handed me flowers and smiled her huge wonderful smile at me. It was a surprise and it seemed to set a somewhat formal tone so I bowed her into the studio. Now I ought to be able to pin down who that was.

At the door had to have been.... Shit, I need to make these names into a deck of cards so I can sort them out. It must have been Mary. Comes out with stress, good humor. I thought maybe Sheila but realized that Sheila doesn't show her emotions. So that was Mary.

And no sooner had she entered the doorway, before I had the door fully closed to shut out nosy neighbors on all sides, than she became someone else. She was suddenly innocent and soft and asked where's my bed. It happened so fast I didn't have time to react to it, and I had to get that door closed and it just passed so fast I didn't see it go.

Now, who was that? Had to have been Marla. Supervising the comforts, the basics. And I am realizing that Marla is easily influenced by some of the other personalities, and is made to do things and say things. I don't think I know Marla terribly well. I don't know enough about her yet to have her precisely placed in my mind.

Pandora walked into my studio—the door is now closed—and on in after asking where my bed was. Before I had a chance to answer, she spoke again, almost interrupting her own self. This one was down to managing matters of form. She wanted to know if I had any tea or wine.

It was awfully sudden. I mean, I hadn't answered her first question yet, she still had her coat and scarf on and I had in mind showing her where to sit and be comfortable. Tea or wine could wait a few seconds longer. Like my attention speaking, when was that, yesterday?

Anyway, who was that leaping out to get her turn? Had to have been Marla, couldn't have been. It could have been Jennifer Moore. She stuttered a little before saying wine, it could have been her age relationship to the wine. It was: "Do you have any tea? Or, or wine?"

I told her the couch opened into my bed and I had wine and could I please have her scarf and coat so she could make herself comfortable on the couch. And I think it was at that moment that a new personality was born, George's wife. It was the first direction she took from me; she breathed out a heavy, "Oh, ok!," smiled, and was already unwrapping her very long scarf. It was releasing control of the situation and taking direction. Or it could have been Mary. But that's it.

She sat and held her wine glass for hours with both hands. She stared into it as she talked. It was Prudence who told me the long sad tale of her life, in a quiet and serious way, protected by her religion from the harshness of the truth.

The evening had a general tone of being quiet and serious.

There were strong magnetic undercurrents going through me and I'm sure through her too, lending an air of importance to the evening, with a delightful feeling about it.

When I hugged her goodbye, she gave me a warm hug at first, and then turned it into a pelvic grinder. She said in my ear, "Um, is there some place we can lie down?" That was Bette Davis.

She wanted to undress in the dark. I could still see her because there were still cracks around the new door that had finally been installed in this shambles of a rooming house, and the hallway made bright streams of light into the apartment.

She screamed when she climaxed and it was so blood-curdling that I slammed a pillow over her face, never slowing down. She struggled to pull it away so she could scream better. So many times I have heard that screaming. I've actually become rather accustomed to it. Who is it who screams?

It has to be Bette Davis. The only other personality listed who has an interest in sex is Mrs. Hyde, and it couldn't be her.

I've slept with almost all of them. It's sleazy, one of my friends told me, to write about sleazy subjects. But I can enjoy small doses of sleaze. It's too interesting not to talk about, because there are distinctly different sexual responses from various personalities, including physical changes.

But I don't need to talk about it now.

There was a lot that happened that night that is only becoming clear to me now. Pandora laid her disqualifiers on the table with me. I didn't bother interpreting that. I am just now realizing that Pandora was engaged in the most important night of her life or lives. She was escaping from the world of the insane to find a foothold in reality. The opportunity seemed absolutely golden to her. I thought I was offering her so paltry a serving of life. I was wrong.

She has led me into the portals of the world of the insane, enough to convince me that it is an extremely horrible way to be alive. Knowing about it impels me to figure out what to do about it. I've been figuring and I'm still figuring.

To her, I was that last impossibility, re-entry into the world of normal people. She leapt at it. I was so occupied with loving her and trying to figure her out and straighten her out that I didn't write a word for three months or so.

We knew about multiple personality back then. She had mentioned it once, along with many other diagnoses or impressions she had been given. But it didn't stand out among the possible explanations of why her behavior was so erratic.

For one thing, just what the hell is multiple personality? What is one personality? I won't bother looking that one up; I need just one answer right now. Let's say that personality is a set of attributes, characteristics and traits associated with a person. The specific combination makes that person recognizable as him or herself. We say things to our friends like, "You don't seem yourself today." The source for my definition is Pandora, what I've learned about personality from getting to know her as deeply as I can.

When Pandora changes from one personality to another, she is still Pandora; she just has a different set of attributes, characteristics and traits, and she is no longer recognizable as the Pandora of a moment before.

Our first week together provides a wonderful example of the disorientation that I've felt in the face of sudden changes. The first week after she moved in, which was actually our second week of knowing each other, had a new playbill every night. The night I'm thinking of was, I think, Wednesday.

After four days of sheer bliss together, she came home from school one afternoon breathless, and standing in the doorway of that tiny studio apartment, facing me sitting at my desk just a few feet away, told me that she couldn't continue our relationship because I've had a vasectomy and she was born to be a mother, and that it was all off.

Needless to say, I was stunned speechless. I can still feel my dropped jaw, my vertigo. It was my first glimpse of Mrs. Hyde. Glimpse, hell, you don't just glimpse Mrs. Hyde. She's all over your ass like tar and feathers once she comes out.

At first we called Mrs. Hyde the Striker because she was so god-awfully expert at it. She knew my weak points like she wrote them, and she let me have it with both barrels, time after time. I never saw it coming, for a very long time. It put me through some very heavy changes.

You can't argue with the bitch because she's always right. I mean, when she pushes my buttons, it's because I've got 'em. She has sent me into absolute despondency over my faults and short-comings, not merely holding them up to my face but showing me how injurious they are to her. You can't deal with shit like that. I had only one course open to me each time, and that was to remedy my fucking faults.

I tried kicking her out once. She was sitting on the couch waiting for a taxi or something. She had her suitcase and bags and boxes all around her, had her coat on and was sitting there scowling, furious. It had been a terrible several days leading up to this, and we'd maintained a high level of hostility.

I sat across from her, waiting for her ride to show up.

189

And I couldn't do it. I said, Pandora, I love you, please don't go.

She immediately became George's wife. I mean immediately. All of a sudden there was no remnant of hostility left. Everything was fine and ordinary instantly. I was so taken back that I had to explain to her patiently that I couldn't do whatever trick it was she had just done, that I needed time to catch my breath.

We don't yet understand at all how the changes happen or what makes them happen. There seems to be some management going on, for sure, but I haven't been able to detect any meaningful patterns yet, myself.

But last night a damned interesting thing happened. Pandora was in bed and I joined her and began to cuddle her. It was Jennifer Moore, and she just wanted to hug and cuddle. So I pleaded, aw come on, be somebody else. And Pandora's face became suddenly serious, she said, I'm sorry, and became somebody else, somebody who was up for making love.

This shroud on my creativity, where did that come from? In my first marriage I felt much too guilty about getting a divorce for a reason like I wanted to start from scratch on my own and prove to myself that I can do it, that my life experience so far adds up to something worthwhile, that I am ready to stand up and test my power of creativity like a man, that I needed this rite of passage before I could feel fully a man.

Instead, I needed to offer something I thought sounded far more plausible: another woman. Why? I felt my life was obligated to my family, that I hadn't been my own man for many years. I have long valued my life, believing it capable of wonderful powers. I had been frustrated by the money demands of being a family man for many years. Today, I pay my bills as soon as I conveniently can and all of the rest of my money is just mine, my power to shape important parts of my reality.

I never felt entitled to what I had. My parents took everything away from me when I earned money. I remember the first time, how shocked I was at the idea, but I was a young child, and I learned that I was to give my money to my parents. And I was deprived so badly during most of my childhood that by the time I was old enough to have any money of my own, it was always far too little to be meaningful to me.

If I come out of hiding, dare to face ancient creditors, will I then feel free to go to the beach? It's a beautiful day, and Lynda and Sandy and Vladimir are already there. I'm here.

I will feel so wonderful when I am rich, having done it on my own, just me and the world's resources I chose to use. No wonder I got frightened one time about the possibility of winning the Megabucks. It wouldn't have solved my basic problem at all, just frustrated it.

I wonder if the dates on those occasional Megabucks tickets I do buy correlate with periods during which my self-confidence is lagging.

Fury has great authority. Fury is fearless and fearsome, bullying and strong. Fury is a power of magnitude.

When fury is channeled into an objective, elements tend to obey. It can be used as a positive force.

Fury was responsible for getting my arthritis under control a decade ago. Fury made a fat tumor on my wrist vanish.

Here is what Rebecca has written recently:

How many times did I ask someone if they knew what day it was? "Orient pt to place and time..."

Do I know what day it is? No, too muddled up right now—huddled under a bridge, shelter from the cold drizzle raining on and off outside without regard to how cold, miserable, and tired I am.

Salvation came in the form of two degenerative men in an old pickup truck. Ending in drunken horror and rape—ripping open my body and my soul laid out to rot and decay.

Screaming, like she was unable to then, screaming in her dreams, twilight sleep with dark shadows lurking round.

It must stop, cease, end, no more pain or disappointment please.

Closest person ever truly loved and cared for—closest friend unable to be my friend—too needy. Good-bye until we meet again.

I want to hate her but I can't. I want to hate my family but I can't—I miss them, instead feeling painful hurt and loss ebbs in and out but never gone.

Trisha cannot be my friend because she is too needy and immature—good-bye until we meet again, never I hope! —Sheila

little girl left alone, Daddy and Mommy too broken to love me, sisters and brothers too damaged, confused, frightened, and guilty to love Rebecca. —Marion

So who loves Rebecca. She loves herself but hates her life. Hates the pain, confusion, disappointment, and loss. —?

She wants to be dead. It hurts too much to go on. God take me home away from awful hurt Let me go —Becka Have to get up and work tomorrow but don't think I can. It's hospital or suicide, can't see in between.

But can't get the hoops together to make this decision.

Dr. N she needs to be in the hospital—but she's too overwhelmed to make the decision

Please help! I can't manage much longer! Call her please! —Marla

Called in sick today, when I woke up this morning with momentary flashes of last night lingering in half sleep state. Desperate lovemaking with George, desperate

193

need to connect somewhere, someone. Undertow of pain and despair—saw myself out in deep ocean waters with undertow pulling me out further away from shore or safety.

Hysterical soundless tears and crying. Crying out to George to please hold onto me. Keep me from slipping away in the terrible waves of darkness.

Visions of yesterday at work—overwhelming screaming demands from pts and staff alike—barely time or space to breathe. I couldn't go into that today—I almost fainted yesterday afternoon from sheer emotional, mental, physical exhaustion, I wouldn't make it today. Body seemed to respond with its own reaction of having a fever most of the morning as if to say it can't take anymore.

Getting rest and perspective—> ending long close relationship with Trisha (6 years, Seth was just a baby when we met with mutual needs and similar situations @ women's group. I grew, changed, matured in important ways—-she did not. Yet some part of me needed her, her lack of giving, lack of friendship—needed to be all giving and nurturing, always understanding while denying own needs for real, genuine friendship. Role model of past relationships —> place in family, caretaker responsible for meeting others' needs while denying my own.

Rainy day brings or brought me back in time to a terrible place and event—a horrible rape that occurred on a rainy desolate day when I was stranded both emotionally and physically, desperately vulnerable.

Thinking of time and date—seemed to happen late June, early July. Enough for now. Tired and numb. —R. Lareau

feeling very fragile, like a translucent egg shell. George yelled at me. I couldn't help crying. I couldn't stop the awful feeling that made the sobbing come out.
—Marion/Jennifer, Marion helped with the words

Horrible waves of panic are washing and rushing over me. A long Holiday weekend, who will be available to help in an emergency? Will I be able to manage working Friday-Sunday? Will I crash and fall to pieces Monday (day off)?

Hospitals are not safe—raped by male attendant and male psych nurse on duty 11 pm-7am, with my history of sexual abuse combined with being patient in hospital nobody would believe me. I escaped from this private hospital to save myself and shredded pieces of sanity. You thought it only happened in state hospitals or state run facilities—not so.

At times it is so bad I can't function, and am dangerously suicidal—the alternative of being in a hospital is terrifying unknowns and nightmares from the past. When she says she'd rather be dead, maybe you'll understand. At home nobody can see how crazy or horrible it gets. That's a two edged sword. I need someone safe and trustworthy to know so that they may help me. I'm in a terrible bind—only decision I've made so far is stick it out here—stay away from hospitalizations. Try to ride out the storm until it clears.
—R. Lareau/Marla

Dr.N—
I will send these to you to read please keep them separate from other writings, because I will need these (and any others sent) back for my journal. You can return them to Rebecca when you see her at next appointment.

Please call Monday when you can (10 am-2pm), she will need your help and understanding, it will be a very bad day. Thank-you.

Call Tuesday nite if not home Monday 6 pm-9 pm —Marion/Jennifer

After the horrible waves of panic hit, I found myself nearly immobile—unable to walk, talk, move freely. Screaming primitive need to curl up tight in a dark corner pouring out with the pain. From a corner of the bed I see George's dark blue sweat suit, somehow they seem to represent some form of safety, security. Managing to slip into them I am able to crawl out towards the stairs—downstairs for some Jack Daniels whiskey on the rocks w/ ginger ok, quick fast acting general pain killer/minimizer.

Can't manage the stairs yet, too overwhelming all the open space downstairs. Crawl under George's desk stay long enough to gather my senses enough to maneuver up into the chair nearby. Sitting there I struggle to manage the uncontrollable sobbing and despair, the screaming urge to slit my wrists wide open while watching life's blood pour out, just like the pain ripping my whole fucking head open with great convulsive sobbing that never seems to end.

Giving physical expression to emotional torment and pain too long suppressed and trapped deep within—letting it all flow out with the gushing flow of my body's blood. Unconsciousness, blackness followed by blessed relief. Crawl back into the bedroom mindless and senseless, subdue crying long enough to call Dr. N's answering machine leave short message of desperate need that can't be answered when I need it. Slide down the stairs bottom first, find the kitchen and whiskey. Gulp down in between convulsive sobs, find myself hidden under a blanket clutching pillow and drink atop my bed.

Sometime later, two thirds of the Jack Daniels consumed from my glass, a numbness settles in enough to get up manage the basics of shower, dress, work-up to starting supper. Hopefully making a presentable sight for George to come home to, not looking like the war-torn casualty I feel so much like. Another day— —Rebecca Lareau

There are painful memories and feelings, fears brought out of the closet to haunt and taunt.

—Invited Diane and Judy (co-workers) to join George and I for supper and drinks. Both agreed wonderful idea, glad to come. One half-hour before Diane and Judy were expected to arrive, Diane calls with some excuse to cancel (Rm mate hurt her back, Diane had to manage that situation-turned out nothing serious, saw her Rm mate the next day at work, looked fine to me.) Judy never bothered to call to cancel—just never came. Birthday party for expectant 8 year old child—all but one guest cancels. The one neighborhood child that does come is a social out-cast with notable handicaps, but a generous loving heart in spite of it all.

Glancing quickly through mine and George's photo album, quick painful glances of past friends truly loved and missed. The price of growth and change is immense at times, the benefits a long time waiting, demanding so much patience and perseverance.

find a person, create a bond of friendship you think will last for always, eroded and erased by change and growth. Like dust it blows away from tight clenched hands hoping to hold on to it.

You tell yourself lasting friendships are possible, transient ones tolerable not right now it's not. It's still painfully out of reach, out of time.

So wait, hold on, continue with growth and change. Continue to wait for its slow revealing benefits. One step at a time, one moment, one day—hold on. —Marla

At last it is weekend.

You can tell from the time that has lapsed that I really can't face it for very long at a time, and I need a special kind of high to sit and write about it.

THE PANDORA JOURNAL

She was Daddy's little girl, all out. Daddy was her world, and he was a wonderful, happy world for her.

Then he sort of turned into a Mr. Hyde and sexually assaulted her. She was four-and-a-half.

Several things resulted. She lost all grasp of the world; it had suddenly been destroyed. She lost all grasp of who she was; her childish identity had been destroyed. She had been terrorized; she had a new standard of horror in her life against which to measure everything else.

A four-and-a-half year old girl who has been stripped of her identity and of her world is in a dilemma, and she was. She sought and created new identities, probably trying out many for the few she selected. None of them satisfied her need to know who she was;

they all seemed incomplete; and so she kept on trying new ones.

Also during those years she endured considerable sexual and physical assault, endured because it was seldom as horrible as that initial event and therefore she knew she would survive it. Her capacity for suffering increased because of her knowledge of the full extent of horror she could survive.

She is now 30 years old and she is my wife. She is a "multiple personality," something I have come to know about from observing her, and it isn't like the idea I had of it based on little more than reading and seeing *The Three Faces of Eve* and *Sybil.*

Her name is Pandora and we have been together for going on three years. So far, we've identified about 16 or 17 personalities. Several of them are very developed and clear-cut; others are fuzzier.

This story is about Pandora and me. It is about me because I am the one who is your witness to what it's like living with a multiple personality. Everything I have to tell is based on my experiences with Pandora, including the things she has told me.

Pandora is the most fascinating person I have ever met or loved. The story of Pandora is of suffering and long-suffering, stress and courage, adversity and determination. You can expect a very multiple kind of story.

Changes are very upsetting to Pandora, and she is going through a number of them now. She is about to quit her full-time job as a nursing assistant and will take off a number of weeks before starting nursing school late in August, after working for two years.

School will bring about a significant change in her status, elevating her to an LPN.

My observations of Pandora have not exactly been scientific. She is not my clinical subject, after all—she is my wife! But I have been challenged by her, over and over, and I love a challenge. I am breezily accustomed to turning life's challenges into accomplishments, after a very long apprenticeship. It had been a long time since I faced a challenge that I truly could not meet. That's Pandora.

My responses to the challenge of understanding her have resulted in much close observation and reflection. I think I know her better at this point than any of her psychiatrists ever has, although I still cannot honestly say, simply, that I know her.

She and I have been through several changes in our three years together. We have lived at three different addresses, plus fourths when we separated for seven months. Looking back on certain times of change, I am wondering if what I see now is something I have seen before.

What I am seeing now is Pandora trying to stir up a flurry of changes, as if to mask the change that is too major to deal with directly. She is striking at our roommate Britt, at her two "close" friends at the hospital, and has already struck at her best friend Harriet.

It has definitely been periodic that she systematically sets herself to severing all of her meaningful relationships. What I don't know is whether those times coincide with times of change. I can probably figure it out if I spend enough time poring through the thousand pages of journal I've written since our relationship began.

She is about fifteen, and is writing notes to Harriet, conducting an extremely polite war on Harriet's sloppy household habits. Harriet is the free spirit type, an artist and ardent fucker. Pandora has personalities with some of those qualities, but I have seen them very seldom myself. I know about them from the tape recorders I hid around the apartment for a month, a story I'll tell you about.

She is fifteen, and is one of those street-toughie type of girls, only it is being restrained to a large extent. She is the classical "poor me" figure, and is completely justified in her complaints, given the particular personality that is offended by them. When she tells me about them, it is with a full soap-opera dramatic delivery, so much so that for a moment I feel like I am watching her emoting on TV.

She is not sexual, especially, when she is this fifteen-year old. I kiss her neck and rub her groin after supper, and we kiss. But she is performing; she has little hunger for it. This is at very great variance with other personalities who have voracious sexual appetites.

Her hand-eye coordination is passable but still youngish. She can pour hot water into teacups with much greater control than other personalities who are older. I try to notice these little things, but so far I have collected what seems to be a super jigsaw puzzle where pieces fit together only sometimes.

Some of these personalities, like this fifteen-year old we call Evaline, can take over for several days running, although they are frequently interrupted by other personalities for brief periods. I sometimes see a parade of personalities, half-a-dozen at a time. The funny thing to me is that I was seeing the exact same parades when we first met, during our very first week together, in fact, and I didn't know what I was seeing. It's not as if I was the kind of man who automatically asked himself each time he met a woman, "Is this woman a multiple personality?" The thought never occurred to me. Pandora mentioned once, in passing conversation, that she once wondered if she had been a multiple personality, but it was such a foreign idea to me that I just shrugged it off. I wasn't the least bit inclined to thinking that I actually knew someone like that; the possibility seemed too far-fetched.

I had to be convinced of it. That happened recently, a few months ago.

Despite the fact that I had taken her to a specialist at Mass. General Hospital for evaluation and diagnosis because we were by that time convinced that she was a multiple personality, and we spoke of it very often, I still did not believe it based on evidence. I was very skeptical for a long time, until finally the evidence had piled up high enough and until a remarkable thing happened.

Remarkably, after almost never daring to face her problem head-on, Pandora suddenly came out with a written list of the names of her personalities and their characteristics.

For me, that list was like providing a set of shelves to a crowded workshop so that everything could be organized and put in its proper place. Suddenly the profusion of various personality behaviors were assignable to specific personalities, and each one of them came to life on that list. I could see every one of them very clearly; I'd been living closely with many of them.

Maybe not every one of them, but most of them. Some of them I rarely get to see, the sexually promiscuous ones particularly. That's something I live with, and for a long time I didn't think it was going to be possible for me.

Evaline isn't a bad kid, just gets tiresome after a while. How much patience can a 45-year old man have with a complaining adolescent? But I know she needs to tell me about it, to unload, to share it with someone and I'm all she has that way so I bear up under it as well as I can.

She's very good around the house, very domestic. She cooks carefully and well, she does her share of the housecleaning, always the greater share. She is a model wife, or at least she is an adolescent's conception of a model wife, sort of based on early TV situation comedies.

The reasons behind her complaints are entirely logical and obvious, but they are based on that artificial set of social values that seldom interfaces with reality. They are all-American early situation comedy values, not matured by experience with reality.

Harriet is usually considerate about housekeeping things, but once in a while she is on a fling and two mornings ago the bathroom and kitchen were a mess when Pandora got up for work. Her towel had been used, and she felt invaded and abused. An earlier incident when the kitchen was left a mess triggered a note and an apology and nothing more. But right now Pandora is cutting off her relationships and I hope she doesn't push Harriet too hard or we might lose a great roommate.

I don't know what makes the personalities come and go, and neither does Pandora. That's the big one to be figured out, because it may provide some leads on how she can control it. In the meantime, her life is a discontinuous miasma hop scotching through time, overwhelming and depressing.

I try to provide some good times for her, and she will usually enjoy them, although to varying degrees. I cuddle and soothe her when she is feeling suicidal. I tell her about experiences I've had with other personalities when she doesn't remember them ("Did we make love last night?" she'll sometimes ask).

Some of the personalities are absolutely wonderful. If it were not for these, Pandora would seem to have no saving grace. No one would put up with her for long if she were limited to her other personalities.

Her wonderful personalities are the more mature ones. There is one that was apparently created especially for me. We call her Gregory's wife. I am not blind to the wonder of having a wife tailor-made especially for me, loving me with a deep and simple love that I marvel over, tolerating my short-comings, catering to my large sexual appetite, and encouraging me in my endeavors.

What man can boast that his wife was created to fit his every whim and desire?

The problem, of course, is that I never know when she is home. I never know who will be waiting for me at the end of the work day. I have to be prepared for anything, anybody. I'm often not prepared, like the time my computer equipment was stolen and she robbed some things from herself to make it look like a burglary instead of a theft by the guy she had picked up on the street. It took me about a year to figure out what really happened.

And then I still don't know for sure. I piece things together as carefully as I can, always being critical of my conclusions, careful to be correct, because Pandora is a real person and I love her and she is in great danger and I need to figure her out so I can know how to help her. We have lived with the danger for so long now, it feels, that we seldom think about it anymore. It's a horrible given that we can't face steadily. But as far as proof is concerned, I have only three sources of information: circumstantial evidence, the things Pandora has told me, and the products of what my mind is able to do with those.

None of that kind of "proof" is either legal or scientific. I have to find my own proofs, and that has been coming from my observations and my thought processes. It is the proof of first-hand experience. The quality of that kind of proof depends on the witness, me. I've questioned so many things about myself that sometimes I don't know whether I am right or wrong. I am alone with this. Actually, I like being alone with it because it is in my nature to face a challenge with as little outside human help as possible.

But it does limit my resources somewhat.

My laboratory for developing an understanding of Pandora has been myself, my only other human psyche available to delve into. This is something I have done most of my life so it is not new in nature, just in degree. I practiced an introspection (meditation) yoga for fifteen years and have studied a wide variety of other metaphysical systems, practicing several. I haven't learned much, but I have learned several things, and that's good considering what a labyrinth the mind is.

Most of my learning has occurred since I met Pandora. I began to mushroom a few years before that, but my new insights into myself have resulted from living with Pandora. My concepts about my mind are not mainstream at all, although they are not unsupported by leading edge theoretical physics and common principles of metaphysics and to some extent psychology. Mostly, my concept of the mind, still far from complete, is based on my study of Pandora and my comparisons between what I see her mind producing with comparable phenomena in my mind.

I've grown a lot, in a strange direction. So this is your witness.

There is the Writer. Mr. Money. Mr. Citizen. The Guru. The Beatnik. The Warrior. The Weakling. The Abuser. All day I've felt like I was about to burst into tears. I finished reading *Prism, Andrew's World* this morning. I've read several case books now—Sybil again, Eve's own story, Billy Milligan. But Andrea emphasized buried memories of childhood traumas, and made me see mine. Andrea best dramatized the actual states of mind of a multiple personality—and I could see mine.

I see my childhood traumas forgotten or dimly recollected with a glossy coating—repression. I see my lifelong forgetfulness— amnesia. I see my inability to voluntarily access parts of myself that I'd like to utilize—disintegration. I see my multiple lives, once simultaneously maintaining several love relationships and needing a shift zone as I moved from one to the other, or serially changing in very radical ways, especially my last major change from Mr. Citizen to the Beatnik.

This is the first writing I have done this year. It has been a long time since I last wrote. Mr. Money has been in charge during this time, developing sideline businesses in a desperate attempt to provide enough income to establish a secure lifestyle and permit full-time writing. So far there are many plans in motion but no income to speak of. And no writing for the duration.

The Writer is able to write but unable to take money responsibilities seriously. In view of this division, it makes sense that Mr. Money take care of the money situation first. But life would be fuller if they could both work at their tasks at the same time.

I don't know if Mr. Money has good judgment, if he is able to assess whether his plans will work. After plunging thousands of dollars into his mail order business, he has learned to launch businesses with the bare minimum possible, and has several that are launchable for about $100 each. I figured one of them out today, though, and it will make money very slowly compared to what Mr. Money has been thinking. I think he is wary of succeeding because then he won't be needed any longer. Right now I don't know who I am. I am a boy crying inside. Nothing I do turns out right. I am doomed to failure; what is the use of trying? My father taught me well by telling me daily that I would always be a bum.

Mr. Money proved him wrong, of course, by making lots of money at one time. But then the Writer fought his way out and changed everything completely. They fought for a long time and nothing got done—no writing, no money-making. I ended up dead broke and bewildered.

The Writer went back to his womb—Boston. He wrote furiously, madly, without control, and produced what he called a novel. It was merely a fight with the Guru, who wanted the book to be his. It turned into an embarrassment.

But I know that the Writer is capable of writing brilliant works. And I even believe that the Guru has a lot of wisdom and esoteric knowledge to share. There is a real management problem, however, in providing adequate opportunities to them both.

So there it is, my very definite handicap somewhat spelled out and recognized.

Preach.

While some truth is left.

Nirvana allures with promises of truth. All truth dissolves into questions.
Who search truth, preach. Preach before all your truths melt.

Who see truth, preach. Preach that there is no truth, only principles of organization.

Preach the principles; it is by way of these that people may follow, and these that they may conquer life.

THE TRUTH IS...THERE IS NO TRUTH

I do not know whether I feel more like bursting into song or into tears. Last night, fearful that one would lead to the other, I drove to a Christmas eve church service so I could sing but never left the truck. I watched the people driving their Oldsmobiles, looking like Methodists. And I drove back to the office.

The office, two rooms at 6312 E. Main in Mesa, is half of my home now. The other half is my pickup camper. These two halves do not equal a whole, however, for Rebecca is gone. I am alone on Christmas day, our special day, anniversary of the day we met, of the day we married. And she is alone, although probably with people. I cannot believe that she is not tearful today. She must miss me as I miss her. She must be questioning what she has done in leaving me. Yet she is even more stubborn than I am, and will probably bury me before noon.

I have missed Rebecca for a long time now, all of the time that we have been in Phoenix, but having her around made it bearable. Now that she is physically gone it is much more difficult and suddenly too real to postpone. I miss her desperately.

Rebecca never landed when we moved here. She felt homeless all along, felt vulnerable and alien, and resorted to Jesus within to the extent that life without became nonessential, including marriage to me. It looks to me as if any excuse would have sufficed for ending our relationship, although there is some sadness in the one she chose, that I refused to become her kind of Christian, the personality that emerged after successful integration of 44 personalities through therapy with a specialist.

Enough of me is so relieved to have the relationship ended that I do not dare take any step toward resolution. I nearly drove to her last night, but wisely had left the address at the office. Then I lectured myself against what I had almost done. I doubt that she will ever be able to trust a man and love him freely. If there were a chance that she could really love me without periodically torturing me and without freezing me out for long stretches at a time, then I would want her back. But I can't expect that from her. It is too much change for one with her background.

Yet, has she ruined me for another woman? Will I ever trust a woman's love for me again? Will I forever be on my guard awaiting the day love is maniacally erased by cannons of hatred? Or if I must learn again myself to trust another, how long will it take? How long is my sentence, my term of isolation?

I am attempting to found and promote my new religion. It is difficult to give myself to it when grief demands so much of me. I am in trouble, and I haven't been able to bring myself around to doing much of anything about it. I tell myself that I need to grieve for a while, then it will be soon enough to look at my troubles. I hope soon enough will not be too late.

My grief makes it difficult to maintain my own faith in my religion. I forget what it is all about, and start thinking it is simply some scheme without substance. I fall badly out of touch with myself. I want this to be over with. I want to be beyond this.

I keep trying to think of replacing Rebecca with a new woman, but each possibility I consider only makes me sad with the realization that there is no replacement for her. My next woman is going to be so different from her, regardless.

I am unfocused. I am in the midst of another great change and it is taking months to pass through. My primary problem is loneliness, yet living alone is also my primary asset. I yearn for a good love life. And I suppose it will come. Meanwhile, I am wasting a lot of my time wishing. My ambitions are piling up. My lifestyle is barely adequate and I want to improve it. My religion doesn't have any developmental direction. My employment situation is minimal. All of these things will improve, but in the meantime I endure.

I lost my wife because I ran out of pot. It's that simple. I wish I could learn to be high—free with my feelings, less restrained in my activities, less withdrawn—without pot. I like myself so much better that way.

The successful integration of Rebecca's 44 personalities posed a major problem for us. Her specialist therapist referred her to a team of doctors for what turned out to be a presentation of her case to an assembly of professionals.

They hospitalized her for ten days which by law they can do at any time, and worked hard to persuade her that this presentation was for her good. In fact, it was

211

for their good, since a case with 44 personalities was unheard of.

Two doctors also met with me to persuade me similarly and to make me promise to have her show up for the presentation of her case. I promised, insincerely.

Neither Rebecca nor I wanted this publicity blitz. I bought a school bus and two weeks later we moved into the bus and escaped to Phoenix.

Her integration was short-lived. It had taken over a year of therapy with the specialist to achieve it, and only several weeks for it to fall apart. We rented an apartment in Tempe. One morning she told me that the devil had been in our bedroom and had moved her barette from the dresser to the other side of the room.

She was her Christian saint personality, the one who spoke in tongues. She demanded that I also become that kind of Christian. She made friends with a neighbor who was similarly deranged and soon gave me an ultimatum: either become a Christian or get divorced.

It was starting all over again. I had tried for seven years to support and help her and it had nearly destroyed me. I simply could not face doing it again. I agreed to divorce and filed the paperwork.

She moved in with some pastor and the last time I saw her was when she accompanied me to sign the final divorce paperwork.

Many months passed with no word about her. Then one day a friend tried to persuade me to make pornographic films and showed me a stack of magazines. Flipping through them, I suddenly shouted, "That's Rebecca! That's my wife!" The page was headlined "Slut Whore Housewife Wants to Fuck Eight Men." It had a Phoenix address that I checked out but it led nowhere.

That was the last I ever heard of her. I search now and then on the web, but she has disappeared. She has disappeared from my life, but not from my heart.

www.ingramcontent.com/pod-product-compliance
Lightning Source LLC
Chambersburg PA
CBHW031508270326
41930CB00006B/311